The Way Back

ALMANAC 2022

WATKINS
Sharing Wisdom Since 1893

The Way Back

ALMANAC 2022

A CONTEMPORARY SEASONAL GUIDE BACK TO NATURE

MELINDA SALISBURY

WATKINS
Sharing Wisdom Since 1893

This edition first published in the UK and USA in 2021
by Watkins, an imprint of Watkins Media Limited
Unit 11, Shepperton House
89–93 Shepperton Road
London
N1 3DF

enquiries@watkinspublishing.com

10 9 8 7 6 5 4 3 2 1

Designed and typeset by Watkins

Printed and bound in the UK by TJ Books Ltd

A CIP record for this book is available from the British Library

ISBN: 978-1-78678-494-0 (Hardback)

www.watkinspublishing.com

Contents

Introduction 6

Introduction

A few years ago, I realized my relationship with the natural world had stalled and was in danger of eroding completely. Often when a relationship stagnates, it's because both parties have begun taking one another for granted and have stopped actively investing in each other. With me and nature, however, the fact that we were on the rocks was all my fault. I was the one making excuses to stay inside; I was the one who'd stopped paying attention to the changing of the seasons, to the wildlife and plants around me, while the natural world continued being as miraculous and strange and beautiful as always.

The problem was that I'd started thinking of the natural world as "other"; something external and beyond myself and my everyday life. Nature had become something I occasionally watched on television, maybe joining in online commentary or calls to action and then moving on with my "real life"; another box ticked, another task done. All of the connection to nature I'd felt growing up, all of that wonder and hope and curiosity, was fading. Meanwhile the climate disaster was worsening and mass extinctions and habitat losses were becoming critical. As the impact of humanity's unchecked greed began reaching the point of no return, I realized I was taking the world around me for granted, even as we moved closer to the brink, and the horror of it shook me to the core.

So I decided to reconnect with the natural world, before it was too late. But how? At the time I rented a room in a shared house, in a town; I had no use of a garden, no easy access to the countryside. I worked in London, commuted, and my spare time was limited; often I just wanted to sit down quietly and do nothing much with it.

I started small. First, I made an effort to go outside and spend time in whatever green spaces I could find; reading, eating, listening to music, or just wandering around. I took photos of anything that interested me, and looked it up when I got home, learning, or rather re-learning, about the world beyond my walls. Then I started growing plants on my windowsills to bring a little nature inside; houseplants at first, moving on to tomatoes, chillies, and herbs as my confidence increased. I went on longer walks, or got buses and trains out to woods and nature reserves, taking lunch and making a day of it. From there I decided to look at my diet and the way I took care of myself, trying to find ways that were better for the planet: locally sourced food, seasonal fruit and vegetables, less plastic, less waste, fewer harmful ingredients.

Everything I'd loved as a child started to come back to me: the wonder of nature, the peace that came from being outside and surrounded by trees and bushes. The thrill of something moving through the undergrowth, the awe that if I sat still and quiet for long enough, animals and birds would wander past me, unfazed by my being there, letting me be part of nature, too.

And it grew. Still it grows, and with it came the idea for this book. A modern kind of almanac, for people who want to connect, or reconnect, with nature but still live 21st-century lives, with all that comes with them. A book that takes into account that these days lots of people live in cities, or share rented homes with family, friends and strangers, or face physical or economic obstacles that make engaging with nature difficult. Something that remembers the folklore of the past, and looks to the stars and the changing of the seasons, but that also centres around practical things normal people can do in their everyday lives to bring a little of the outdoors indoors. Something with an eye on the future, and what we can do to champion and appreciate the natural world.

I'm maybe not what most people think of when they imagine a naturalist, but that's what this book is all about:

breaking down those barriers and realizing anyone, anywhere, with however little time, can be a naturalist, because the only things you really need are a love of and curiosity about nature, and a desire to connect with it, learn about and be grateful for it. And that makes me exactly the right person to write a guide that will take you through the whole year, because I've lived it. I'm still living it.

To make it easy and fun to use, the almanac is divided into the twelve months of the year, and then further sections within.

Each month starts with a note; the weather, the mood, things you might see if you go outside. Then the skies; the phases of the moon, the movements of the planets, meteor showers. The next section talks about gardening you can do even if all you have is one windowsill, and guides you month by month with what you should do, and what to expect. There's a section about seasonal produce, which includes a recipe I love. All the recipes are vegan, because I am, but feel free to substitute dairy ingredients if you wish, or add meat or fish. A lot of the recipes for meals have also been purposefully written to make just one or two portions, because there's nothing more annoying than finding a great recipe only to realize it's intended to feed a family, or to make multiple portions to be stored in freezer or fridge space a lot of us are lacking.

There's a section about the home, and how you can make it a better natural environment for you to live in, and also how to bring nature inside for the days and weeks when you can't go outside. How you can use your phone to learn and record your journey, how you can create little indulgences or swap out old ones for newer, more natural and sustainable ones.

There's a book club section, where each month I recommend a fiction or non-fiction title that spoke to me about nature in some way; maybe the landscape, maybe the journey, maybe the story of change and growth. If you want to talk about the book, or meet your fellow Way Backers, I'll be using the hashtag **#WayBackBookClub** on Twitter and Instagram to talk about them, so feel free to join in or start your own strands of thought.

My favourite part is the Voices section, which includes some of my favourite folklore and folk practices from the past, and an interview with someone in the present, a person who, like me, is re-navigating or forging their relationship with nature, overcoming any obstacles and using whatever means necessary to do so on their terms. It was such a privilege to gain an insight into how other people are rising to this challenge, and I hope you find as much wisdom in their words as I did.

Finally, there is a journal section, for you, so you can record your thoughts, feelings and adventures as you go along. It's up to you how you read and use this almanac, but I'd recommend taking it month by month, setting aside an hour or two to read through and start making plans.

One final thing to note is that I am British! As you read through, you'll notice that in addition to discussing the natural world in the UK, I also talk a little about nature in the US, and I think it's important for me to make it clear that I don't live in the US, and never have. Everything you read about nature in the UK is my lived experience; it's drawn from years of amateur study, observation and and exploration, so it comes from a place of authenticity. But to write the parts that relate to the fauna and flora of the US, I've had to rely solely on research, and the help of a US biologist. I've done my best to try to get it right, but the US is so vast and ecosystems, climates, habitats, plants and flowers vary so much from state to state – and sometimes even within states – that it's inevitable I've missed things that to US readers might seem obvious, or commonplace, and for that I'm sorry.

All that remains is to wish you good luck on your way back to nature. We're going to have a great year.

January

Regarding January

So here we are. January. The festive season has passed, leaving dark days and darker nights, dreary weather and, for a lot of us, little to look forward to. It's possible that guilt about overspending, overeating and overdoing it during the festive season is creeping in.

Then there's the pressure to begin reinventing ourselves, to, at the stroke of midnight, cast off our vices and become healthier, thinner, more successful, wealthier, more worthy of love, more appealing to get followers and likes and social media validation. All of these things we're told are what we need, what we have to become, if we want to be happy. You'll notice all of the things we're supposed to acquire and become all fit a narrow and artificial, wealthy, white and western bandwidth of what "good" lives should look like. And they don't factor in the natural world at all.

At a time when the natural world is still regrouping and gathering its strength, we're punishing ourselves for who we've been and pushing ourselves to become someone else entirely. We're trying to force delicate, nascent shoots out of depleted, undernourished soil and they will not thrive.

So, I'm giving you permission not to succumb to media and brand demands to change yourself. I forbid you from ANY great acts of change at this time. These dark days are

ideal for nurturing and soothing, for resting and recuperating.
No matter how you spent the festive season, it's likely to have
taken a toll on your emotional and physical reserves, and
January offers the perfect time to refill your well and plan for
the future. It's a good time to start keeping a journal if you
don't already, to set out your goals and hopes for the year
to come.

However, we're not entering total hibernation. We need to
remind ourselves there's life beyond walls and computers.
We must begin rewilding ourselves.

The idea of rewilding is daunting at first; many of us won't
have deliberately sought out nature in a long time, perhaps
some of us never had the chance to, through no fault of our
own. For me the way back to nature has been a homecoming,
not an introduction, but I appreciate that's not the same for
everyone, and I'm happy to be the one to gently usher you
outside, to meet what I hope is going to become an important
and necessary part of your life.

But in January though…? Who in their right mind would
encourage you to go outside then? January is notoriously
bleak; grey clouds hang too low, the sun hidden behind
them, nothing more than a faintly glowing white disc. The
wind bites, the air feels too thin, and the weather is cruel
and capricious, driving you back indoors. At best rain, at
worst snow…

I want to invite you to think about snow. Perhaps,
like me, you can remember when it still snowed fairly
regularly in winter. When you wake up earlier than usual,

because the light is different. Snow light is a luminous thing, making the world fairy-tale strange. Snow covers the familiar, blurring out the details of the world and making everything anew.

Then there's the crunching underfoot of fresh powder, and the glee and power of being the first person to tread on it. You are an explorer, an adventurer – the old, familiar paths are covered; you must make new ones. You are forging a new way forward; you are choosing where you go.

Snow quietens the world, sometimes making it seem as though you might be the only person left. It stills traffic and travel, silences everyday hustle and bustle. It's easy to listen in the snow. Easy to hear. Close your eyes and open your mind to the world around you. What do you hear?

This is your January. An open, clean space that you can navigate as you see fit. A quiet space where only the most necessary sounds are made. The world, for you, for now, is covered in fresh snow.

If you're feeling very eager and it's possible for you to do so, you can devote a day, an afternoon, or at least an hour or two to getting outside, snow or not. Bundle up toddler-style, unable to put your arms at your sides because of the layers of jumpers and scarves and coats, pull a hat over your ears and venture outside. The sun will be pale and gauzy, the wind will drag sharp teeth over any exposed skin, and the ground beneath your feet will be either unyielding or boggy, but none of that matters. What matters is you go and seek signs that it won't be dark forever. Look for snowdrops, one of the rare plants to thrive in winter weather; look for the crows and magpies and other birds who still have business to do.

If getting outside isn't possible, why not take an hour to explore some webcams and see what's going on in the places we don't normally get to see. For UK wildlife and nature, try the *Countryfile* webcams list: www.countryfile.com/wildlife/wildlife-webcams-uk-ireland/, which includes land animals, birds, and even seals, or the Wildlife Trusts webcams list: www.wildlifetrusts.org/webcams. You might find some of them have forums in which you can compare notes with other viewers if you want to, or if you're active on Twitter and Facebook, try searching for groups or tags, or start your own conversations if you'd like to discuss what you're seeing and learning! And for readers in the US, or those who want to look at nature in the States, try searching for national park webcams. The Katmai National Park brown bear cam is famously brilliant, especially over summer when the bears are hunting salmon; it's the home of the Fat Bear Week, the tongue-in-cheek online contest that "pits" the bears against each other to see which has put on the most weight for winter. Or try searching through the cams featured on www.nps.gov/subjects/watchingwildlife/webcams.htm for golden eagles, volcanoes and more!

Then put the kettle on, and congratulate yourself. Your journey back to nature has begun.

In the skies

Our first new moon of 2022 comes 18:33 GMT on 2 January, making the beginning of the month both celestially and traditionally an excellent time to begin again.

January's full moon has many names: Wolf Moon; Ice Moon; Old Moon; the Moon After Yule. The most commonly used moon names – and the ones this almanac will use – originated with the Algonquin tribes, and they traditionally applied the name to the entire lunar cycle, not just the full moon. The names were chosen in reference to a common occurrence or event that happened during that cycle. The Wolf Moon was so named because it was the month during which wolves would howl with hunger. 23:48 GMT on the 17th gives us our first full moon of 2022.

We can also expect the annual Quadrantids meteor shower on the 3rd and 4th. At its peak you can expect up to 40 meteors per hour. And we're lucky that the new moon will still be a slim crescent and will set early in the evening, offering excellent viewing conditions, so long as the skies remain cloudless. If you have an app on your phone like Star Walk, use it to find the constellation Boötes and keep an eye on it, as the meteors will radiate from there.

Meteor showers occur when the Earth in orbit passes through the debris that comets and asteroids leave behind as they pass through our solar system. It's when this debris collides with our atmosphere that we see what we call shooting stars.

For all "In the skies" sections I have given the exact GMT times of each celestial event. These can be adjusted by adding or subtracting the number of hours' difference in your part of the world (including BST). This could move the event forwards or backwards one day. Through the night-time is usual to view planets, except Mercury, which may be visible just before dawn (Western Elongation) or just after sunset (Eastern Elongation). Note that these elongations are measured east and west of the Sun, not the direction you are looking!

Logically, we all know making a wish on what is essentially space trash is unlikely to yield results, but at the same time there's part of us that always keeps one eye on the sky in case the chance for a wish happens. For centuries people saw celestial events as harbingers and predictors of the future, and if it does nothing else, wishing upon a shooting star offers us a glimpse into what our truest desires are. To decide in that split second what it is we want most urgently and to confess it to the sky.

So, while I make no promises about the results of wishing on stars, I hope you'll take the chance this month to look skyward and really interrogate what it is you would wish for if you could, because that's one of the seeds you'll begin planting next month. We might not be able to magically manifest our hopes and dreams into reality, but knowing what they are is a great place to begin.

In the soil

If you were tempted to skip this section because you don't have a garden, or you have access to one but you're not allowed to grow things in it, you don't need to worry, because this part of the almanac has been especially written to cater to growing things in pots, on windowsills, and largely indoors!

It's not about yielding a bountiful harvest to feed you through winter, or starting a commercial enterprise. It's about nurturing something from seed to plate, and watching it grow and change from nothing to something. It's as much about observing the cycle as it is about benefitting from it, and taking your place in the cycle to see something through. But nature does love efficiency, so why not enjoy eating your own fresh, homegrown produce at the same time?

Your first task is to think carefully about what you'd like to grow. There are many different varieties of vegetables and fruits available these days, including hybrids and miniature ones that grow well in pots. The best and easiest are **tomatoes, chillies, radishes, baby carrots, spring onions (scallions), salad greens, microgreens, dwarf beans** and **peas, basil, chives** and **rosemary,** all of which can be grown successfully in pots, on patios, balconies or even windowsills.

While you're choosing what to grow, as well as thinking about what space you have, think about the flavours you love, and visualize yourself growing and caring for the plants, harvesting them and using them in your cooking. If it's possible, then take a trip to the library or to a garden centre for a dose of old-fashioned research, or stay tucked up at home and use the Internet to explore the kinds of things you'd like to grow that will work in the space you have.

Some of my favourites include **Tiny Tims (tomatoes), Tom Thumb dwarf peas** (you might be noticing a theme), **Little Gem lettuces** and **radishes** (avoid larger ones like daikon, but

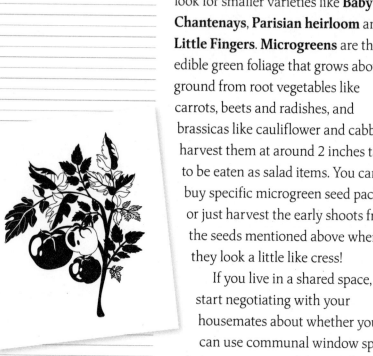

regular radish seeds are good). **Carrots** are very accommodating vegetables too, and will cheerfully grow in pots; look for smaller varieties like **Baby Chantenays**, **Parisian heirloom** and **Little Fingers**. **Microgreens** are the edible green foliage that grows above ground from root vegetables like carrots, beets and radishes, and brassicas like cauliflower and cabbage; harvest them at around 2 inches tall, to be eaten as salad items. You can buy specific microgreen seed packets, or just harvest the early shoots from the seeds mentioned above when they look a little like cress!

If you live in a shared space, start negotiating with your housemates about whether you can use communal window space or balconies to grow things. To begin, figure out what direction your windows face, and which rooms get the best/most light for what you plan to sow. Tomatoes and herbs like a lot of sun, so a southwest-facing window will please them. They will need protecting from bright sunlight when they're little, and if you have them outside on a windowsill or balcony they'll need protecting from the frost, wind and inclement weather, but small greenhouses or cloches (transparent plastic or glass domes) for individual pots are readily and cheaply available online or in shops like Flying Tiger Copenhagen and Wilko (in the US, try Target, Dollar Tree, Walmart, etc.) – or you can use household jars. Peas and beans can get tall and will need staking, so vertical space is important if you want to grow those. Lettuces and spinach do well with very little direct sunlight, and are best grown in troughs as they need wide, long spaces, although I have had success growing spinach in individual 20cm pots – lettuces and spinach grow fast and their roots are shallow, which is good news for the container gardener! As a rule, any fruit or vegetable that grows from a flower will need lots of sun; leafy greens will do best in shaded areas, and root veg like partial shade. Kale is great for the shaded, container gardener – try Dwarf Blue Curled.

Check List:

- ☐
- ☐
- ☐
- ☐
- ☐
- ☐
- ☐
- ☐

For now, your job is research and planning: cajoling your housemates into letting you occupy the windows, thinking about the kinds of containers you'll need for the space you have, whether that's inside or outside, and, when you're ready, ordering or buying the seeds you want to grow. Please don't feel under any pressure to grow masses – if you just want to grow one basil plant, that's fine too. Choose what you think you'll be able to give the most attention to.

In season

Though we're now deep in winter, you might be surprised to know there is a huge amount of fresh fruit and vegetables seasonally available. We tend to think of summer and early autumn as the seasons where harvests are the most bountiful, but good, fresh produce is available for most of the year round – there are only a couple of months in late spring when the pickings are naturally slimmer.

Beetroot (beets), **Brussels sprouts**, **cauliflower**, **celeriac**, **chicory**, **Jerusalem artichokes**, **kale**, **kohlrabi**, **leeks**, **parsnips**, **potatoes**, **salsify**, **shallots**, **swede (rutabaga)** and **turnips** are all in season through January.

Fruit-wise you should easily be able to find **apples**, **rhubarb**, **blood oranges**, **clementines**, **kiwi fruit**, **lemons**, **oranges**, **passionfruit**, **pears**, **pineapples**, **pomegranates**, **satsumas** and **tangerines**.

When the line between night and day is blurred and the cold seeps into your bones, the best cure is a massive bowl of hearty soup. Apple, celeriac and rosemary soup is full of sweet, warm, nourishing flavours and perfectly seasonal – this recipe makes two or three generous portions.

Apple, celeriac and rosemary soup

Ingredients

1 tbsp vegetable oil

---

1 medium-sized yellow or white onion, finely chopped

---

1 garlic clove, finely chopped or crushed

---

1 tsp dried rosemary

---

1 bay leaf

250g / 9oz hard green apples (Granny Smiths are ideal!), cut into small chunks. The sweeter the apples, the sweeter the soup will be.

---

1 medium-sized celeriac (around 400g / 14oz), the skin removed and cut into small chunks

---

2 pints / 40fl oz / 5 cups vegetable stock

---

1 tbsp lemon juice

Salt and pepper

Optional:

1 tbsp dairy-free crème fraiche / cream
A handful of chopped walnuts

Method

1. In a large pan, heat the oil, then fry the onion on a medium heat until soft and translucent. Add the garlic, rosemary and the bay leaf, then fry for a further minute or two (do not allow the garlic to brown!).

2. Add the chopped apples and celeriac to the pan and cook gently for 3 minutes. Then add the vegetable stock and lemon juice, followed by salt and pepper to taste. Simmer for 40 minutes, or until the celeriac and apples are very soft.

3. When they are, fish out the bay leaf, then use a hand blender or stand blender to blend the soup to a smooth liquid.

4. To serve, stir in 1 tbsp crème fraiche / cream per bowl, and sprinkle with the chopped walnuts.

Serve with thick slabs of fresh bread.

In the home

In keeping with our plan to be indulgent and kind to ourselves this January, our first task of the year is to create a comfortable, cozy place in our homes we can hide away in when we need some time to ourselves. Almost everything in nature has a den, or a nest, or a safe space it can retreat to when the weather is foul, and you should be no different.

The idea is that, with a few props, which can be changed year-round depending on the temperature and your needs, you build a "den" for yourself as a place to go when you need a little TLC. It should be somewhere you can go to read, or journal, or have a cleansing cry, call your loved ones, nap, meditate – whatever you need to do to let go of any tension you've been holding.

To begin, you need to choose a space in your home that you can adapt into a personal sanctuary – if you live in a shared house, it can be a corner of your bedroom, or even your bed. The focus isn't on the physicality of the space, and it doesn't need to be permanently set up for use; over the years mine has been on various beds, a yellow chair, and is currently a particular corner of my sofa.

When I've had a rubbish day, or the skies are grey for what feels like the hundredth day in a row, or I'm exhausted from socializing and commitments, I gather my kit together and build my cocoon, and I invite you to do the same. Below is a list of items that you might find helpful in creating that sense of care and indulgence.

- **A blanket or throw** of some kind to wrap yourself up in. In autumn and winter I like thick, chunky knits, and items with texture – fake fur and velvets are lovely and tactile, while in summer a thin cotton waffle is nice.

- **Candles, for a cozy, gentle light.** If you're not a fan of candles, or you live in a rented property that doesn't allow them, consider investing in a lamp that emits a warm, soft light – Himalayan salt lamps are lovely (please be aware, though, that they're not suitable if you have pets). If you do choose candles, be sure not to choose paraffin-based ones unless you're in a well-ventilated space.

- **Something scented.** This can be candles, allowing you to combine light and scent, or incense, wax melts, an oil burner, or even a few squirts of your favourite perfume on the blanket or throw.

- **Something to eat or drink.** Herbal teas are a fast and easy favourite – pick a tea that is unique to the time you'll spend in your cocoon, and reserve it just for then. If you're not a lover of herbal teas, then consider another drink, or snack, that can become synonymous with the time you spend there.

- **A soundtrack.** I like to use the sound of rain (even if it's raining outside!), but you might prefer a crackling fire, a beach, or a playlist of your favourite songs – anything you can put on low in the background to mask the everyday noise of dogs barking, traffic, neighbours or housemates, the central heating gurgling, etc.

What we're trying to create is an immersive experience that both stimulates and soothes the five main senses, bringing you feelings of relaxation and happiness within your cocoon. Over time, your mind will start to associate these sensations, smells, tastes and sounds with the feeling of being relaxed and cared for, and you'll be able to use them to quickly put yourself in a mental state where you are calm and at ease.

In your phone

Because one of the things we're going to start (or continue) doing this year is looking at events in the night sky, it's a good idea for us to try to familiarize ourselves with it, at least a little. Before the advent of technology, this would have involved star charts and compasses, which would have been challenging enough, without the added hindrance of modern light pollution blocking out the starlight (not to mention having to stay up all night, every night, to observe them!).

Luckily, we have easy access to a variety of tools and apps we can use to help us map the skies, and I recommend downloading one and learning how it works this month – after all, if you're lucky enough to live in an area with low light pollution, on a clear night you can stargaze without needing to leave the house! I am a big fan of Star Walk 2, and use the fully paid bells-and-whistles version, but there are plenty of free stargazing apps available; try SkySafari, Star Tracker, SkyView, or simply look in your app store. I find with apps that it's usually best to try out a few and see which one you prefer using, especially if you're thinking of paying for one. So take January to try a few on for size and see which you like best.

People have always contemplated the stars; before they were used for travelling, or reading the seasons, they were stories. Ancient people looked up and saw figures and animals – serpents, gods, horses, heroes – and now we can too.

In caring for yourself

A few years ago, I did an audit of all the disposable plastics I brought into my home to see if there were areas where I could feasibly cut down, or cut out, my consumption of them. The biggest area by far was cosmetics, grooming and hygiene – makeup, hair products, cleansers, moisturizers and so on – so I decided to find ways to switch them out for products that came in glass, or cardboard, or were "naked" instead. At the same time, I started to think carefully about what exactly I was putting on my skin and hair, and whether there were adjustments I could make there too. After some research I started swapping out products and, in some cases, making my own replacements.

This recipe for nourishing body butter is one of them. The only "rare" ingredient it requires is raw shea butter, which can easily be bought in various weights online and even in some chemists, and a few of the indulgences in the almanac use it, so you won't need to worry about it going to waste. A lot of the recipes I've included use the same ingredients in various combinations. You can also simply double the quantities of either butter rather than using both, if you'd prefer – some people don't enjoy the naturally smoky scent of shea butter, and others dislike the chocolatey aroma of cocoa butter, so please do choose what works best for you.

Nourishing Body Butter

60g / 2oz shea butter

60g / 2oz cocoa butter

60g / 2oz coconut oil (unless using odourless coconut oil, you may detect a coconut scent in the finished product)

60ml / 2fl oz / ¼ cup sweet almond oil

2 tsp arrowroot powder / cornstarch (this is optional, but it makes it less greasy on application)

20-30 drops of your favourite essential oil

Clean and sterilized jar

1. Place a heatproof bowl in a large saucepan full of hot water on the hob, keeping the water warm but not boiling. Add all the ingredients, except the essential oils, to the heatproof bowl and allow them to melt together – be careful not to let any water get into the mix.

2. When blended together, remove from the heat and

allow to cool, then place in the fridge until the edge of the mixture is beginning to harden.

3.   Using a stand blender, or a hand blender, whip the mixture until it pales (it will turn from toasty yellow to cottony white) and becomes light and fluffy. This may take up to 15 minutes, so if you're using a hand blender make sure you have something to support your arm! If you find it isn't turning white, then it's not cooled enough – return it to the fridge for 10 minutes or so, then try again.

4.   Once the mixture is whipped, add the essential oils, fold them into the butter and decant into your sterilized jar. If you keep water and other contaminants from it then it can last up to a month in a cool, dark place!

One final thing to bear in mind is the natural scent of the butters. As mentioned before, raw shea butter has a smoky, nutty odour, and cocoa butter smells like chocolate, so factor that in when you choose your oils!

In writing

For the first ever **#WayBackBookClub**, I've chosen a non-fiction book: Amy Liptrot's **The Outrun**. Published in 2016, it's a memoir about Amy's struggle with alcohol abuse while she lived in London and how she moved back to her childhood home of Orkney to confront her addiction, and in the process rewilded herself. It can be hard to read at times – Amy is brutally honest about her past, and owns up to her behaviour in bleak, unflinching terms, but juxtaposed with her confessions are heart-stoppingly beautiful moments in nature: her work for the RSPB cataloguing Orkney's population of corncrakes; when she discovers her joy in sea-swimming, exploring shipwrecks and having encounters with seals.

It feels hackneyed to say, but it appears at times as though Amy Liptrot had to lose everything to find herself. In Orkney, Amy has to live a life that's slower – sometimes frustratingly so – than the one she had in London, but she finds the pace suits her. It's a book about finding balance, and learning to live with uncertainty. Most of all, it's a book about someone who finds her way back to nature, which I think makes it the perfect inaugural book for us.

As you read, I invite you to think about times when you've felt uncertain, or unbalanced. Explore what you might need to settle and centre yourself. Be gentle with your feelings, and your fears, and your heart. Practise living slowly, even if it's just for an hour a day.

Voices, past and present

The days around the new year are ripe with superstition, lore and ritual about things you should and shouldn't do to protect or attract your luck for the coming year, particularly on New Year's Eve and New Year's Day. You can take it all with a pinch of salt – after all, the first of January is only the beginning of the new year in some cultures, and calendars are not fixed: the Roman calendar was only ten months long before Julius Caesar added two more months, and though the Gregorian calendar we follow today was introduced in 1582, it wasn't adopted in the UK until 1752, when the legal new year began on 25 March. Time is a slippery, mutable thing.

But, if you feel you'd like a little extra luck, or a few hints about what to expect, here are some of my favourite New Year's superstitions and rites, to help you begin the year the best possible way:

- One of the most popular sentiments is that whatever position you find yourself in as the clock strikes midnight will continue through the year – hence why kissing is such a popular activity.

- Make sure both your cupboards and wallet aren't bare to ensure they won't be in the coming year.

- Open all of your doors and windows just before midnight to let the old year out and the new one in.

- Don't let anyone from your household leave on New Year's Day without letting someone in from outside first. Traditionally, a tall, dark-haired man (bearing gifts!) is best.

- Always wear something new to begin the new year.

- No cleaning or laundry of any kind on New Year's Day, to keep from washing or sweeping your luck away.

- Save any tears for 2 January – crying at the new year indicates you'll spend the coming year crying too.

- In Spain, one ritual is to eat a grape for every stroke of midnight for luck. It's also tradition to wash each one down with Cava – and apparently isn't as easy as it sounds, to the point where people practise in the weeks leading up to 31 December!

- Repeating "White Rabbits", or simply "Rabbits!", as the first words you say at the beginning of any month is a commonly known superstition, though no one knows quite where it came from. It appears in a 1909 periodical called *Notes and Queries*, in which the author mentions that their children – and other children – say it, but never explains where it originated. Like all superstitions, it's grown since, taking on a life of its own as it's been handed down.

I find superstitions and old wives' tales fascinating. I love that even in these science- and technology-heavy times, so many of us still hold to these routines or beliefs that, if we follow them, might keep us safe, or bring us luck, or predict our futures. I like that a little of our old, nature-worshipping selves still exist when we count magpies and recite verses that could be spells, or predict the coming weather based on the colour of the evening sky. I like that we still look to the natural world around us for clues about what will happen next.

As I mentioned briefly in the introduction, each month will introduce you to the voice of someone who is navigating, or re-navigating, their relationship with nature, and the first Voice (which might be cheating a bit) is my own.

My relationship with nature began when I was a child. I think when you're a child, nature feels more of a home to you than most indoor or human spaces. Maybe it's an innate curiosity about the world simply because everything is new to you, or a need to find a place in it that doesn't always bend to the usually incomprehensible ways of adults. Somewhere you can be wild and rebellious. From toddlers digging for worms in the mud, to older children lying flat on their bellies staring at rivers, ponds or lakes for a glimpse of fish (or, if they're very lucky, a frog), children and nature are deeply in cahoots with each other, and so it was for me.

I was fortunate in where I grew up. My family lived on a sprawling, crowded housing estate, but it was bordered on all four sides by farmland, woodland and fields. All the better for someone like me, who was obsessed with animals. I wanted to pet everything I saw, wanted desperately to befriend it. For a long time my aspiration was to be a vet, because it would mean getting to spend time with animals every day.

My obsession was so deep that I started an animal club, of which I was the only member – possibly because the objectives of Animal Club were to learn the Latin names of every native mammal in the UK, what their tracks looked like, and also their stools. It wasn't the kind of hobby that made you cool and popular, but I didn't care (I did a bit, but not enough to stop). I spent a lot of time outside on my own, hiding in woods I'd been forbidden to enter, on my belly fishing newts out of a pond I wasn't supposed to go near, sneaking off to the fields as the sun went down in the desperate hope I'd see a fox, or even a badger.

I didn't actually see a wild fox in real life until I was an adult; an urban one, slinking down the street like a streak of dirty orange light. And I saw my first wild badger during the writing of this book – it turns out there is a very active sett just around the corner from where I live; I can see them every single night if I choose (at first I chose that a lot, now I give them a break from my staring).

Like a lot of the other people I interviewed during the course of this book, I lost my love of nature around the time hormones, and later, responsibilities and expectations kicked in, and assumed that wild, curiosity-filled part of my life was over. But then a few years ago, the need to spend time outside began to grow once more. It kept growing, until I had to do something about it, and when I finally did, it felt good. It *feels* good. I feel like I'm my best self when I'm tramping through a wood, or clambering over a rocky beach, or harvesting wild blackberries. Nature makes me feel small, but in a good way, because I'm part of something extraordinary and so much bigger and stranger and bolder than me.

I think it's something a lot of people are feeling these days. As the news highlights the climate disaster and the consequences of our consumerism, as the icecaps melt and species go extinct and forests burn, we're all becoming aware that this resource – which should be infinite, if used conscientiously – is actually running dry, that we're milking it dry, and it's already too late to reverse some of what we've done. I believe it's making many of us want to return to a life where we live more synchronously with the natural world. For the first time in a long time, we're aware of the earth and our relationship with it, and we want to fix it. And we can, if we try.

In your hands

February

Regarding February

I always feel a bit bad for February, because aside from Valentine's Day (and Pancake Day!) mostly all we seem to want from it is for it to be over. By February we've reached our limit for grey and cold and wet and we're craving something that puts a little spark in our step.

It's out there, if we go looking. Still fragile and tentative, and still at risk from frosts or storms, nature is poking her head out of the ground, and so we should too. This month, if we're able to, we're going to brave the weather and put on coats, gloves, boots, scarves or whatever else we need to feel prepared and we're going to go on our first real exploration of the natural and green spaces around us.

One of the ways February's interviewee, Emilie Lyons, recommends is to begin by searching online to see what green or wet spaces were near her home. Most county and local councils will have a website dedicated to the natural resources in the area, whether that's woodlands, nature reserves, canal paths, wetlands or parks, and it's an excellent place to start your investigation. Or you can look for wildlife trusts. Sit down with your phone or a computer and plot an outing to one of the spaces near you, paying attention to getting there and back, and any potential hazards you might face because of the winter weather (and, in the US, from wildlife – here in the UK our biggest land predator is the European badger, but in the US you have bears, cougars, coyotes, wolves and Bigfoot[1] to consider).

Try to get outside two or three times this month, and try to visit the same place. Being out in daylight, however weak, is good for your circadian rhythms, and the more time you spend outside, visiting the same places, the more they will become familiar to you, and the more you'll notice when they start to change. Of course, if you want to mix up your travels and explore new places, that's up to you – if that's what makes you feel a connection with nature, then that's all you need to do – but don't underestimate the benefits and joy you'll get from noticing how the same landscape changes every week as the seasons unfold. If getting out isn't something you can do, then this is the month to pick a few favourite webcams or live feeds that you'll follow through the year, marking the changes that occur. You could also pick a view from a window and make it your own.

If you do go outside and decide to retread the same paths, maybe figuring out a favourite walk, then be sure to take your phone so you can make a record of it. Each month in the "In your phone" section of the book there will be a way to use the technology you have to improve and enhance your relationship with nature; the simplest way is taking photographs of the things you see, and how they grow, blossom and change.

---

1. Reports on Bigfoot's existence are unsubstantiated, but it's always best to keep an eye out, I find.

Things to look out for in February in the UK are crocuses, daffodils and narcissus, early bluebell shoots, wood violets (which smell as pretty as they look) and long catkins on alder trees (allergy sufferers, I'm sorry to say this is your first warning that tree pollen season is approaching). In the US, look for the disarmingly named skunk cabbage in swampy areas, red-flowering currant in the Pacific northwest, satin flowers (also known as Farewell-to-Spring) in California, and the Indian plum, or Osoberry, beginning to bud – native to the Pacific coast, this is one of the earliest plants to have leaves. Songbirds will begin putting on their best performances too, ready for the mating season, so keep an ear out for blue tits, blackbirds and song thrushes, especially in the UK. In the US, listen for the American goldfinch across the south, chickadees (the tit family in the UK), red-winged blackbird and the pine siskin. (Something worth noting is bird populations will vary from state to state, so it's a good idea to spend some time figuring out what's local to you.) If it's a mild February, you might see bumblebees having a tentative forage, or even early ladybirds. Deep in their setts across Britain, badgers will be having their cubs, and in the skies of the US, American bald eagles are enjoying the end of their mating season. Bald eagles favour breeding grounds near large stretches of water and tall, dense, mature forests, and breeding pairs will return to the same habitat year after year; their aerial mating displays are unforgettable.

Little signs, little signs. Spring is on the way.

In the skies

Pleasingly (if you are like me and enjoy when things line up neatly), February begins with a **new moon at 05:46 GMT on the first of the month**. And though I wouldn't claim to be a practitioner of any particular New Age – or even ancient – religion or practice, I do try to align some of my activities and commitments with the moon phases, if for no other reason than it adds structure and rhythm to my month, and makes me feel more connected to the natural world.

The new moon represents the start of the moon's waxing, which is to say getting fuller, making the new moon an ideal time to sow seeds, plan new beginnings, and open doors and windows for future possibilities. I like to take the first few days of the month to think about what the next four weeks will hold for me and what I'd like to achieve, welcome and say goodbye to in that time. As the moon waxes I try to keep my energy focused on beginning and continuing new projects and ideas, starting new rituals and habits (like yoga in the morning, meditation before bed) and getting things ticked off my to-do list.

The full moon, at 16:56 GMT on 16 February, represents to me the height of my energies for the month. It's when I'm hopefully beginning to see results from all the things I began two weeks earlier. Then, as the moon wanes (becomes less full), that's the time I think about what's not working and say goodbye to it. It's a good time to banish negativity from your life, and to finish projects, as well as cleaning and recycling.

February's full moon is also known as the **Snow Moon, and sometimes the Hunger Moon,** both of which originate with Native American cultures; Snow Moon, as it was usually in February when the heaviest snows fell, and Hunger Moon, because those selfsame snowfalls made hunting difficult.

In the soil

During the first week of February, it's time to source the pots, containers and saucers you'll need to begin your garden. Make sure to get pots with drainage holes in the bottom – plants left sitting in wet soil with no drainage will be prone to developing root rot and may fail to grow. A pot with holes in, set in a saucer or tray, is the best way to ensure you don't overwater. And as this month's Voice says, you don't even need to buy pots; you can recycle old margarine or ice-cream tubs by thoroughly cleaning them and making holes in the bottom for drainage.

You will need to buy potting mix, and to that end, make sure you're up to date with your tetanus boosters – you need to have five doses over the course of your lifetime for immunity, the last one usually happening at age 14 as part of the 3-in-1 teenage booster, but if you've never had it, or you can't remember the last time you had one, check with your nurse or GP to discuss if an extra booster is needed. I am someone who likes to put my hands in the potting mix and fill pots that way, but if you're concerned about that you can pick up gardening gloves quite cheaply, or just use tools – I don't own a trowel, but I do have a set of old soup spoons put aside for the purpose!

Something to remember is that if you're starting your seeds in trays, or small pots, you'll need larger ones for when they grow, so don't be afraid to buy or save bigger pots for the future. You'll want to grow your plants in the largest possible containers to give them room to grow, and to prevent them from drying out.

PLANTS YOU CAN SOW THIS MONTH: Spinach, chilli varieties, microgreens.

Spinach: If you're sowing into seed trays, fill with potting mix and poke holes around 1.5cm deep with the handle of a spoon, or a pen, every inch apart in one single tray, or one per individual tray. When they get to around 2 inches tall, repot into larger pots or troughs. If you're sowing directly into pots, fill with potting mix and poke holes every 3–4 inches apart, and the same distance from the sides. Place one seed in each hole and cover over. Spinach prefers cooler weather, loves shade, and likes a lot of water and food.

Chillies: You can start your chillies in a pot, by filling with potting mix and poking a hole around 1.5cm deep and planting one seed per hole, then covering over. Most chillies like sunlight and heat

Check List:

- ☐
- ☐
- ☐
- ☐
- ☐
- ☐
- ☐
- ☐

in the day but cooler temperatures at night. They can also grow very tall, so consider the variety you choose carefully – miniature versions are better if you're short on space.

MAINTENANCE THIS MONTH:
Nothing yet!

HARVESTING THIS MONTH:
Not yet!

In season

February sees bananas back in season. I'm sure you will know both of these facts already, but in case you don't, bananas share around 60% of their common DNA with humans and around 95% of bananas in shops today are genetically identical to each other. That's right – they're clones, from one specific Cavendish banana plant, because modern bananas are seedless, and therefore sterile! They're also in grave danger from a fungus that causes a wilting disease called Panama disease, and scientists are working to find a way to help them repel it, so they don't go the way of their predecessor, the Gros Michel banana.

Also still in season are **rhubarb**, **blood oranges**, **kiwi fruit**, **lemons**, **oranges**, **passionfruit**, **pineapple** and **pomegranate**.

And for our vegetables we have **Brussels sprouts**, **cauliflower**, **celeriac**, **chicory**, **Jerusalem artichoke**, **kale**, **leeks**, **kohlrabi**, **parsnips**, **salsify**, **shallots**, **swede (rutabaga)** and **turnips** still readily available.

There's something about February that's often worse than January; though it's shorter, it's rarely sweeter. Which is why it's wise and necessary to add our own sweetness. Luckily for us, bright, tart citrus fruits are still in season, which makes February the perfect time to make a sticky orange polenta cake. It's best eaten on the day of baking, so either share it with friends and loved ones, or put on some trousers with an elasticated waist, grab a fork and have at it. No one has to know unless you tell them.

47

Orange polenta cake

Ingredients

125g / 4½ oz polenta (cornmeal) (loose; not the pre-cooked variety)

150g / 5½ oz plain (all-purpose) flour

100g / 3½ oz ground almonds

2 tsp baking powder

125g / 4½ oz white sugar

Zest of 3 oranges

Pinch of salt

60ml / 2fl oz / ¼ cup orange juice, from fresh oranges

120ml / 4fl oz / ½ cup non-dairy milk (I use soy for cooking, but oat would also work well)

60g / 2¼ oz melted vegan butter

For the syrup:

200ml / 7fl oz / scant 1 cup water

100g / 3½ oz white sugar

60ml / 2fl oz / ¼ cup orange juice, from fresh oranges

Method

1. Preheat the oven to 180°C / 350°F / gas mark 4 (use the rising heat to melt your vegan butter in an oven-safe dish or bowl) and grease a 25cm round cake tin. Set aside.

2. Add all of the dry ingredients – polenta, flour, ground almonds, baking powder, sugar, zest and salt – to a large bowl and mix them together.

3. In a separate jug or bowl, mix together the wet ingredients – orange juice, milk, melted butter – until well blended. Then add this slowly to the bowl of dry ingredients, mixing steadily, until you have a smooth batter.

4. Pour the batter into your greased tin and place in the oven. Check it after 30 minutes by spearing it with a clean skewer, toothpick or knife (or the thin end of a chopstick, which is what I use). If it comes out mostly clean, you can remove the cake from the oven to cool. If it's still very wet, pop it back in for another 10 minutes.

5. While the cake is baking, it's time to make the syrup. Add the water and sugar to a pan on the hob and bring to the boil. Then add the orange juice and allow it to simmer and reduce until it has thickened and roughly halved. Allow it to cool until warm.

I like to pierce the cake all over with a toothpick to allow the syrup to drizzle inside. I also add pistachios and dried rose petals to the top if I'm feeling fancy. This actually goes a long way to offsetting the elastic-waisted sweatpants in terms of glamour, too.

In the home

This month is one of four when we're going to look at ways we can bring the natural world into our homes, to remind us it's out there waiting on the days when we can't get to it. Part scavenger hunt, part crafting session, your goal in February is to venture outside and harvest materials you can use to create something beautiful and natural for your home.

I'm not going to give you any particular instructions; what you can find and make is entirely dependent on where you live, or where you go, and how imaginative, crafty and time-rich you are. The important thing is that you go outside and find things that you like, and that you can repurpose or arrange in a way that makes you think of the beauty of nature. The only rules I will give you are to stay clear of private property, not to take anything rare or threatened, not to damage anything, and to please try where you can to gather things that can easily be replaced, or already have been – stones, fallen sticks, etc.

If you don't have a lot of time and/or live in a very urban area or by the sea, maybe what you're going to bring home is a stone or rock you find beautiful – if you've got the time/ the inclination, perhaps you'll even paint it. Or maybe you'll bring back a few and glue them to a circle of thick cardboard or a plastic food container lid to make a simple holder for pillar candles.

If there are trees nearby, maybe you'll find some interesting twigs. Let them dry out and arrange them in a small glass or jar. If you're feeling arty, you could try wrapping them with embroidery floss or colourful wire; they look lovely in an arrangement, but can also be used to make statement jewellery! Or why not gather a whole bunch, glue them to an empty jar, cut them level with the top if you prefer, and you've got a rustic-looking pen pot?

Bark rubbings or leaf rubbings are an option, too, if you're happy to embrace your inner child. Using artist's chalk you can create some very moody, avant-garde pieces. They can be framed if you're especially proud of them, or glued into scrapbooks or the "In your hands" section of this journal. Or you can even find leaves to bring home and draw.

This is very much up to you. Go out and keep your eyes open. Don't be afraid to use your hands to touch and feel and make. Bring nature to you, find ways to repurpose it and bring it into the home.

In your phone

In February, we're going to do the first of two clean-up sessions of our technology. I am a firm believer in cleaning sessions working in tandem, because unless you have supernaturally strong powers for getting rid of things, it's likely you keep some things back, promising yourself you'll use them, but maybe (probably) you never do. By having clean-up sessions in two parts, with a chunk of time between, you get to actively test this promise and know if the stuff you saved was worth it.

The same rules apply to our phones, e-readers, laptops and all of our tech. So, this month, take a little time every day to go through your personal technology and figure out what you need to keep and what you can afford to say goodbye to. Old contacts, old apps, old photos. Maps, recipes and instructions you downloaded, used once and forgot about, pictures that your phone saved from other apps.

On your computer, go through old bookmarks and get rid of the ones that don't resonate with you anymore, look in your document and download folders for forms and receipts you downloaded for posterity but are no longer useful. Take it further and look at your social media –

which apps still have access to it? Maybe it's time to remove some of them. Maybe it's also time to delete the guy you went to school with who keeps sharing weird conspiracy theories too? And unsubscribe from those emails that you never open anymore.

On e-readers, seek out those book sample chapters you downloaded but still haven't read – now's the time to fondly wish them well and delete them. Books you didn't enjoy and won't reread – send them into the ether.

If you come across anything you're not sure about, make a note of it, either here, in this month's "In your hands" section, or somewhere else, so you can revisit it later and decide whether it gets a final reprieve. And remember to back up any files that are important, by using cloud storage, emailing them to yourself, or whichever way suits you best.

In caring for yourself

This month we're going to consider if there's anything we use in our beauty and hygiene routines that we could swap for more environmentally friendly alternatives. We're lucky to live in a time where we can buy products that are suited to our individual skin-

and haircare needs, but many of the products available contain chemicals and ingredients that are damaging to the environment, and which simply haven't existed long enough for us to understand any long-term effects they may have on humans. And, depending on our skin types and needs, a lot of them can be swapped cheaply and easily for basic alternatives that don't do as much harm to the natural world. Here are a few of my favourites.

Coconut oil to remove makeup: I buy it in a glass jar so the packaging is more easily recycled, and use a small glob, massaged into my face, to remove all of my makeup, including eye makeup. I clean it off by gently using a fabric face flannel and hot water to pat, not rub, the oil away, repeating until it's thoroughly removed and then following it with my usual face wash. It can also be used as a moisturizer, but bear in mind coconut oil is comedogenic (which means it clogs pores), so it isn't recommended for people who are trying to manage acne.

Apple cider vinegar to rinse hair: A couple of years ago I stopped using regular shampoo and conditioner and switched to bars as one of the ways I could cut down on my plastic consumption, which meant putting my hair through a tricky transition phase as it got used to being cleaned with much milder products.

After some searching online, one way I found to help my scalp adjust was to use a scary-sounding acid rinse, which is one part apple cider vinegar to five parts water, poured over my hair and massaged into my scalp, and then left for 5–10 minutes before rinsing it out. It left my hair soft and detangled, and very shiny, and I've kept it up weekly even now my hair is used to the new routine. ACV can also be watered down and used as a toner, or alongside water in dry clay mask mixes. Please don't use it neat on your skin or hair; it is acidic and will strip the natural moisturizers you have there. Please also be aware it isn't suitable for every skin type, and you should patch-test first. And of course take care not to get any in your eyes!

Beer can be used as a hair rinse too: It is now used by numerous haircare companies as an ingredient in conventional conditioners because of its ability to leave hair incredibly shiny. As with ACV, be sure to rinse it thoroughly from your hair, and a dark stout is best – let it go flat before you use it and dilute it with a little water.

A final rinse is rice water! Whenever I cook rice I save the water the rice is rinsed in and any left over from cooking and allow it to cool, before using it as a post-shampoo rinse next time I wash it (though not during the same washing session as the ACV rinse). I massage it into my hair, then wrap it in a towel for 20 minutes before washing it out. If you have very fine or porous hair, or lots of baby hairs or regrowth, then rice water isn't recommended as a rinse as it's very protein-rich and could cause a protein imbalance in your hair – again, test it first on a small section of your hair to see how it responds. If you have a dry scalp or hair, or suffer from dandruff too, it's also best avoided.

One thing to note: it's important to tread carefully when replacing conventional ingredients with natural ones – your skin and hair will be used to the ingredients they know, and it will take time for them to adjust to the lack of chemicals, and the new chemistry of the natural ones. If you are managing any skin or hair conditions or complaints then please speak to your GP or dermatologist before changing your routines or introducing new things to them. And begin carefully: less is always more, and patch testing is key. If your hair is dyed, highlighted or chemically altered, please be aware the chemicals in the dye may react adversely with some natural ingredients. Never use anything new on your skin or hair without completing a patch or strand test 48 hours beforehand.

In writing

February features the book club's first fiction title:
Hannah Kent's _Burial Rites_. It's the story of life in a rural
community in Iceland, set over winter 1829–30. It's going to
be the last winter that Agnes Magnúsdóttir ever sees,
because she will go on to have the dubious distinction of
being one of the two last people publicly executed in Iceland.

Though you may worry I've spoiled the book for you,
Agnes (and history) make her fate clear from the beginning.
And what follows isn't quite the bleak story that the premise
suggests, but one of hope and tolerance, compassion and
forgiveness. One that asks for the cold and dark to stay a
little longer because the return of the sun also means an
ending that can never be undone. It's a story about a woman
who strives to be better than she "should be" and who faces a
terrible punishment for it.

It's very possible it will make you cry – I cried when I first
read it. The story of a community opening up in the literal
darkest and coldest time to embrace not only an outsider, but
someone accused of murder, and destined to be punished for
it, is a beautiful, generous and selfless thing.

Aside from the human message of the book, the writing
of weather and landscape is beautiful. _Burial Rites_ is a love
letter to the strangeness of Iceland compared to what we
know: the black sand beaches and active volcanoes, the hot
springs and the northern lights. Iceland is a country used to
cold and dark winter months and its people are accomplished

at bringing light – both literal and figurative – into their lives to combat the winter, and we can learn from that. To fight the darkness we need to make light – of our own, and with other people. I guarantee by the end of the book you'll be ready for the sun, and to come out of hibernation.

Voices, past and present

In early February 1855, villagers across Devon went to bed as snow blanketed the countryside. The following morning, they woke to a world that was white and gleaming… and found something, or someone, had been abroad in the night. More than 30 separate locations, from Topsham to Teignmouth, reported waking up to strange, hoof-like footprints in the fresh snow. It could easily have been attributed to horses, or other hooved animals, had the prints not covered houses, haystacks, rivers, barns – anything in the path of the footprints was simply walked over, as though whatever made the tracks had no trouble leaping on top of buildings or treading across roofs. Popular legend has it the Devil himself walked through the Devon countryside that night.

One of my favourite stories about the Devil in British folklore takes place in Wales, at the Devil's Bridge, a place I visited with Emilie Lyons, this month's Voice.

Once upon a time, the Devil visited Wales, as he'd heard it was quite beautiful. While on his travels, he came

58

across an old woman by a river, who was crying. When the Devil asked what was wrong, she pointed to the other side of the river, and the Devil saw a cow there. The old woman told him the cow was hers, and she'd swum to the other side and the woman couldn't get her back.

The Devil offered to build her a bridge to get to her cow, but the price was the soul of the first living thing that crossed the bridge. When the woman pointed out that that would be her as she went to fetch her cow, the Devil smiled. That was his plan.

After giving it some thought, the old woman agreed, and the Devil sent her home while he got to work.

The following morning the old woman returned to the bridge, her faithful dog yapping at her side. Sure enough, there was a bridge where there hadn't been one before. The Devil had kept his word.

"Now it's your turn," he called, expecting her to cross the bridge, and thereby forfeit her soul to him.

The old woman stepped onto the bridge. Then, quick as a flash, she took a loaf of bread from her skirts and threw it to the other side. And her dog chased it.

The Devil was furious; the dog was a living soul and the woman had promised him the first one to cross the bridge was his. Outraged he'd been outwitted, and refusing to take the soul of the dog, he vanished. The woman collected her cow, and all three creatures went home, very pleased with themselves.

Emilie Lyons, a theatre dresser from Powys in Wales, is my best friend, for the purposes of full disclosure. So I already know how much she loves nature and the outside world, because we've done a lot of fun outdoor things together: watching red kites feeding in the Elan Valley, looking for dinosaur footprints in Hastings, traversing Epping Forest for hours, just to see what we can see. But something Emilie has recently gotten into is gardening, which has been challenging as she lives in a third-storey flat and has no access to a traditional garden. Instead, she's made one, using pots.

She's always been very outdoorsy – a former Girl Guide and Girl Guide leader, growing up in a town in the middle of Powys, surrounded on all sides by farms, valleys and woodland, she had little choice but to embrace a life lived in close contact with nature, and it's something she always seeks out, especially since she moved to London for work.

"I live very close to Epping Forest, so I escape to it whenever I need some thinking time; I rely on nature a lot for that. But also for fun! I think when we talk about relying on something, especially for our physical or mental health, it's easy to let yourself think of it as a kind of duty, when actually it's also a nice thing to do. It's fun to go out and see what wildlife I can see daily; I've downloaded a few different apps – including a birdcall app to help identify what birds I hear, and the Forestry Commission's tree-identifying app – and it's fun to have things like that to do."

Emilie also swims regularly at Kenwood Ladies' Pond, the closest she's come so far in London to replicating the wild swimming in rivers and brooks that she grew up doing.

So, growing her own fruit and vegetables is not such a huge leap for her, but living in a flat share in London has made it slightly more challenging. The answer, Emilie found, was growing things in pots using the space she had, and concentrating on things she would eat: radishes, kale, spinach, chives, and – for the challenge – cucamelons. Her dad is a gardener, growing runner beans and tomatoes and things like that, but this is the first time she's taken charge of growing things herself.

"I bought seeds and pots and soil. I've got windowsills and a tiny patch of concrete outside the flat I can use."

As well as having the benefit of being an extra connection with nature, and supplying her with fresh, organic food she can trace back to seed, it also provides her with an incentive to step outside in summer, something she doesn't enjoy.

"I hate hot weather, and given the chance I'll just stay inside. But having the plants means I have to go out to check on them and water them, so I have a reason to go outside for at least five minutes each day and get some sun."

To anyone who wants to build their own relationship with nature, Emilie has the following advice:

"Apps. Get apps. There are loads that will help you identify plants and trees and insects and mushrooms; anything you spot while you're out. And look for local groups and wildlife trusts too; there's loads of information on what's in your area. I was recently poking around on my local wildlife trust website and found out about a wetland reservation that I'd never heard of before. No matter where you live, there's always something near you."

She also wants to make it clear that to grow your own food you don't need much. "I think people fall into the trap of thinking they need loads of specialist stuff to do it. But all you need is seeds and soil. You don't even need proper pots – you can take plastic tubs out of your recycling and make holes in the bottom; to start seeds you can use mushroom trays from the supermarket, or make little newspaper pots. An old spoon works to shovel soil. You pretty much have everything you already need – just add seeds, soil and a windowsill."

February

In your hands

March

Regarding March

Two years ago, the world collectively experienced the longest, strangest March I think most of us can remember. Before then, January and February were the months that always seemed to outstay their welcome, but March 2020 lasted eons. What should have been a month of hope and growth and exploration became a time of fear and restriction and forced hibernation. Winter went on too long, even as the weather outside turned golden. Beyond our walls the natural world thrived without traffic and pollution and the human influence encroaching on it. People said at the time that birdsong seemed louder, and shared photos of wild animals roaming places they would have been too scared to explore before: wild boar in suburban streets in Italy, jackals photographed in parks close to joggers in Israel, and dolphins venturing into harbors across the world. In the UK, the Great Orme Kashmiri goats came down to roam the streets of Llandudno, charming people online (though conflicting reports suggest this might have been in response to very bad weather).

It was wonder in the midst of horror; nature is often both. And we craved it. We couldn't stay away from parks and woods and beaches, stealing moments to pause and turn bare faces to the sun, heading outside for exercise we'd previously preferred to do in glossy gyms to thudding music. Necessary confinement made us think about what we were missing when we were indoors, glued to screens. We yearned to rediscover nature. Which is what this book is all about.

I hope whatever has come to pass, we haven't forgotten those few months when we realized what had been right before us all along. I hope we're still eager to use the energy of the vernal equinox, and the growth and flowering and nesting we see in the natural world, and that we harness it to forge our own new beginnings.

When I was growing up, my grandmother used to recite a folklore proverb – "March winds and April showers bring forth the sweet May flowers" – which now I think means we're supposed to brace ourselves against the inclement weather of this month, and the next, in order to reap future rewards. But I never saw the wind as a bad thing! I don't know about you, but winds always make me feel mischievous. The rational, adult part of me gets cross at how they muss up my hair, blow my skirts up, rattle my windows and shake the trees, but something inside me feels a pure, primal glee as the wind gets up. It makes me think I could fly, that I could fling myself into the gust and soar. I like when the wind gets behind me and pushes me onwards. I love how I can lean back in a strong wind and allow it to hold me up for a moment. Then it whips away, and I either fall or right myself in the nick of time. The risk is the price I pay for being cradled by the wind, and it's worth it.

That's what we're going to do this month. If we stay indoors, we're going to think about our breath, and how we can use it to blow out flames, to soothe burns and cuts, to warm our hands. A little breeze of our own that is a tiny force of nature. Take a few moments to breathe deeply. Breathe loudly. Breathe onto your window and draw shapes in the condensation. Find a sleeping animal on one of the webcams and breathe in time with it for a few minutes. Light a candle and blow it out. Relight it and do it again, from further away. Make a wish if you want to – why wait for birthdays?

And if we go outside, we're going to take a beat to remember the March when we couldn't. Then we're going to find the wind and let it push us onwards, let it hold us up for a moment. We're going to trust it, and ourselves, in that moment, and the moment after, when the support is gone. We're going to hold ourselves up, and keep walking.

One word of caution: if you're going to be travelling through pasture, woodland, long grass, ferns, or anywhere you think sheep or deer might frequent, please wear long trousers and invest in a tick-removal tool; March to June, and again in August to October, is tick season, and some can cause disease in humans. If you are bitten, remove the tick as quickly as possible without squashing it. You might also want to carry a small plastic bag or pot with you to store the tick in; in the unlikely event you do fall ill after a bite, the tick can be tested to help speed up a diagnosis.

Things to keep an eye out for in March include frogs!

This is the month when things get amorous for amphibians, and so if you can get to a pond, it's possible you'll see – or more likely hear – them there, performing their hearts out to attract a mate, and there might even be even some frogspawn too. In western US listen out for Pacific chorus frogs. Though the frogs that live in the west tend to be less vocal than their noisy eastern cousins, the Pacific chorus frog, as the name indicates, is an exception – the stereotypical "ribbit" sound we associate with frogs comes from them! March in all humid regions of the US is the beginning of salamander season too, since they are coming out of hibernation now to breed. In fact, the Appalachians are one of the biggest hotspots for salamanders in the whole world. So, if you're lucky, after a decent rainfall you might catch a glimpse of one.

In the UK, March hares are a typical sight; if you can get out to farmland or meadows you might see males "boxing" with other males in a bid to keep them from mating with nearby females. If the weather is mild, you might just see hedgehogs coming out of hibernation; adders too. Foxes will be giving birth to their cubs, and as the weather warms, badger activity will increase as they forage to feed themselves and their growing young. If the winter has been mild and dry then the bluebells will be out in force and even the most practical, pragmatic person will feel a bit of fey glee walking through a woodland carpeted in bluebells. It's also wood anemone and primrose season, and who isn't cheered by a soft, butter-yellow sun beaming up at you from the ground?

In the US, it's the beginning of breeding season for raccoons, and coming up to the end of the mating season for both beavers and striped skunks. It's likely the majority of skunks you see on the move this month are males – the lustiest among them can cover up to 4km a night looking for love! If you live near the west coast, March is the ideal time to observe the spring migration of the grey whale, and if you live near bear habitat, be aware the black bear is beginning to come out of hibernation.

Almost everywhere insects are starting to emerge in full force. You'll spot bees and even early butterflies on warmer days – mayflies too.

We did it, we made it to spring. Another winter survived. Good job. Well done.

In the skies

This month sees the **new moon occurring at 17:34 GMT on the 2nd**, with the **full moon following at 07:17 GMT on the 18th.** March's full moon is predominantly known as the Worm Moon, though it's also called the **Lenten Moon, Crow Moon** and **Sap Moon**. Despite the often-negative associations people have with worms, we, as emerging champions of nature and budding gardeners, know better. Worms are a vital part of the ecosystem, composting waste and creating new fertilizer from it, improving and oxygenating the soil as they travel through it, as well as taking their place on the food chain – which is where the name **Worm Moon** comes from. At this point in the year the frosts stop and the ground thaws, bringing worms to the surface, and therefore attracting the attention of birds! The Worm Moon is a sure sign that spring is on its way to the northern hemisphere, and is usually the last full moon before the vernal equinox.

In the soil

For us northern-hemisphere dwellers, the outside world is beginning to awaken in earnest, ready to begin anew – just like we are! This year the vernal equinox will happen on **Sunday 20 March, at 15:33 GMT,** marking the official beginning of spring in the northern hemisphere (and autumn in the south).

PLANTS YOU CAN SOW THIS MONTH: Strawberries, tomatoes, Little Gem lettuces, spinach, microgreens, spring onions (scallions), peas.

If all you have is a windowsill, seek out cherry tomato seeds like the Tiny Tim variety – I've had great success growing them on my kitchen windowsill for three years running now, alongside my own basil. Throwing them onto a salad feels like a tiny piece of magic every time. You'll need small to medium-sized pots – I start mine in tiny ones and then repot as they grow – and you should invest in sticks and jute string to help stabilize them as they grow. Tomatoes don't need pollinating to grow fruit, but they do need lots of light if you want them to ripen.

As with the chilli plant seeds from February, sow **tomatoes**, **spring onions (scallions)**, **strawberries**, **peas** and **lettuces** in seed trays or small pots by filling with potting mix, and then making holes to deposit the seeds in, before covering over with more potting mix. Keep them somewhere light and warm as the shoots come through. Repot when they get to around 2 inches tall – and label them! Lots of plants look similar when they're young.

Tomatoes, strawberries and peas love warm, sunny weather, so keep them somewhere they'll get lots of that. **Lettuces and spring onions (scallions), like spinach, prefer cooler and shadier spots.**

Microgreens: Sow multiple seeds into your pots. Space doesn't especially matter for them, as you're harvesting the green tops, not the roots, or the vegetables that would come later, so

Check List:

- [ ]
- [ ]
- [ ]
- [ ]
- [ ]
- [ ]
- [ ]
- [ ]

you can be quite liberal! Microgreens need 12–14 hours of light once they start to grow, so wait until after the spring equinox to sow them. Once you start, keep a rolling supply by adding more seeds week by week to the same pot, as they'll grow and become harvestable at different rates.

MAINTENANCE THIS MONTH:
Keep an eye on your chillies – they'll need to be potted in bigger pots when they reach 2–3 inches tall.

HARVESTING THIS MONTH:
Nothing yet!

In season

Spring is the sparsest season for harvesting; compared to summer, autumn and even winter, there's very little ready to come out of the ground, or off plants. It's the last hurrah for the citrus fruits, so take advantage of **oranges, blood oranges** and **clementines,** and also prepare to bid a seasonal – if not commercial – farewell to **passionfruits** and **pineapples. Bananas, kiwi fruit** and **rhubarb** remain in season and will stay so through May.

Vegetable-wise, it's time for the last of the **cauliflower, kale, leeks, salsify** and **swede (rutabaga),** while **purple sprouting broccoli** and **spring onions (scallions)** come into season.

To make the most of the last of the lemons, my recipe this month is sunshine in a jar. When I was little, lemon curd on toast was one of my favourite things to eat – the bitter bite of the lemon, the smooth sweetness of the sugar. The lemon curd tart was always my favourite too, and when I became vegan I thought I had to say goodbye to lemon curd forever. But a nostalgic search online revealed dozens of recipes for a veganized version, and after experimenting with a few of them, I was able to come up with my own foolproof version. It takes minutes to make and will keep in the fridge for a week, but if it lasts that long I'll be disappointed in you.

Luscious lemon curd

Ingredients

3 large, unwaxed lemons

3 tbsp cornstarch

100ml / 3½ fl oz / scant ½ cup cold water

200g / 7oz white sugar

60ml / 2fl oz / ¼ cup sweetened soy milk

70g / 2½ oz non-dairy spread

Method

1. Pre-heat your oven to 150°C / 300°F / gas mark 2. Wash a jar large enough to hold 450ml of liquid in hot, soapy water. Rinse, place on its side on a baking sheet, and then put it in the oven to sterilize.

2. Meanwhile, zest and then juice the lemons. Place the lemon zest and the cornstarch in a stainless-steel saucepan and gradually pour in the water, whisking gently until it forms a paste. Then add the lemon juice and the sugar, and place the pan on a medium heat, whisking throughout.

3 Continue whisking until the sugar has dissolved and the mixture is smooth. Then stir gently until the curd is satisfyingly thick.

4 Turn the heat down low, and add your milk and dairy-free spread, stirring all the while. When the milk and spread have been fully incorporated into the mix, your curd is done!

5 Remove from the heat and (carefully!) take the now-sterilized jar out of the oven. Pour the curd in while it and the curd are still hot, and seal.

The curd is delicious eaten warm from a spoon, and while still liquid is perfect drizzled over vanilla ice-cream, but for the traditional lemon curd experience, leave it in the fridge overnight to set and enjoy it the following day thickly smeared on toast.

In the home

The spring equinox is upon us, and that means it's time to spring-clean! I like to have a good clear-out twice a year – in March and September, timed with the equinoxes. They're great opportunities to check in with yourself and think about how much you've changed and grown over the past six months, as well as to gently and gratefully shed anything in your life that isn't serving you anymore.

A good clear-out can be daunting, so we're going to break it down into smaller, manageable sections that you can tackle over the course of a week, and accomplish around your other commitments. One tip I would give you is to think about the timing of your clear-out – it's likely you'll have items you want to donate to charity shops, or to recycle, or things that might have no further life or use, in which case you'll want to think, prosaically, about your local waste collection services, and when you can take things to charity shops. Feel free to restructure the plan to suit your needs.

Day one: We'll start off gently with makeup, toiletries and medications. It's time to throw out any open makeup that you either haven't used in at least six months, or that has been open for longer than advised on the label. We know that makeup can be a breeding ground for bacteria, and we're not helping ourselves by holding on to it. Thank it for its service and send it on its way. Recycle what you can. The same goes for old toiletries and medicines.

Tubes of Deep Heat that expired in 2020 can be disposed of, as can the facewash you tried twice and didn't love, and the sun cream you opened once but never used again. If you have anything in date that hasn't been opened but feel you won't use, consider donating it to a local foodbank or shelter. Anything that has been opened but you just don't love could be passed on to willing friends (assuming it's still in date and it's hygienic to do so). Remember to wash all of your makeup brushes, hairbrushes and combs, and any cloths or reusable pads you cleanse yourself with. Think about treating yourself to a new toothbrush – there are multiple bamboo options available, even heads for electric toothbrushes. Change your towels.

Day two: Time to look at your clothes, accessories and shoes. By now we're all familiar with the six-month rule (if you haven't worn it in six months, get rid of it), and the Keep, Donate, Bin model. But I'd like to add a fourth option: Repurpose. There might be items you can't donate because they are stained or have holes, but there might be a way you can reuse them somehow! Old, clean tights can be used to store onions and garlic; old knickers, T-shirts and skirts can become dusters and cleaning rags. Old dresses could become cushion covers, or patches could be cut out to repair throws. The Internet is absolutely full of ideas for upcycling old garments, so after you've sorted your clothes into the "keep", "donate", "bin" and "repurpose" piles, why not grab a drink and do some research on exactly how you can repurpose those "spare" items?

Day three: If you're a reader, today is the day we're going to look at our books. I'm not saying there's an amount you should or shouldn't keep, but I am gently suggesting that, if you know in your heart of hearts that you have books you're never going to read, finish or read again, maybe it's time to release them into the wilds of a second-hand shop to free up space for books you will read, finish and read again. If you can't bear to, then you can take the rest of the day off and feel no shame or guilt. Books are lovely.

Day four: We're going to sort out our paperwork. Unless you need them for work or your tax return, it's time to get rid of any old receipts. If you still receive paper statements for your banking and utilities, consider converting to online account management – it'll save paper and offer you instant access and control over your accounts. Put everything in order, and if you don't already have one, make a note to pick up a box file to put everything away in one, easily searchable place.

Day five: Time to go through all of your knick-knacks and everyday items – cups, plates, cutlery, cookware, Tupperware and storage, throw cushions, blankets, ornaments, everything that isn't actual furniture – and decide what to keep and what to give away. Follow the rules as before: if it has any value to you then of course you should keep it. But if you could cheerfully live without it, it's broken or no longer fit for purpose, let it begin a new life somewhere else.

Day six: Cleaning part one. This is the deep clean – scrubbing toilets, sinks and baths, washing skirting boards, door and window frames, etc. Take down your shower curtain if you have one and give that a wash. Use a vinegar wash (I use one part distilled white vinegar to four parts cold water and add a drop of lavender essential oil) on tiles, mirrors and shower screens. Dust and hoover all the fiddly places you usually neglect. Go through your food cupboards, fridge and freezer, and see what's out of date, or what's close, or what you suspect you won't eat and make alternative plans for it. Clean the shelves and drawers.

Day seven: Change your bed sheets. Dust, mop and hoover as normal. Check over any plants, prune where needed, feed and water if necessary. Take your recycling, donations and rubbish to the various collection points. Then come home, have a cleansing bath or shower, put on clean pyjamas or nothing at all and get into your fresh bed. Everything is orderly; right now you love everything you have and it serves you completely. That's a joyous thing.

Contact List:

- [ ]
- [ ]
- [ ]
- [ ]
- [ ]
- [ ]
- [ ]
- [ ]

In your phone

After last month's phone clear-out, it's likely you'll have come across some names that you haven't thought about in a while, or that made you feel a *little* guilty because you're long overdue a catch-up, or you still haven't replied to their last message.

So that's the goal for this month: reach out to people you miss, those you haven't spoken to in a while, and see how they are and what they're up to. Be mindful – if it's been a long time since they've heard from you, they might not want to talk anymore and it might be time to put that relationship out to pasture. And that's OK, because at least you know you can joyfully delete their information to make room for new friends yet to come.

Whether you do this online, via messages, phone calls or even a good old-fashioned postcard is up to you, but take a few pauses this month to reconnect with some of the neglected people in your life.

In caring for yourself

March belongs to Pisces, most watery of star signs, and so this month we'll take to the water to indulge ourselves – particularly salt water. Salt has had huge significance for almost as long as humans have existed: as a spiritual and literal cleansing agent, as a healer and a preserver. And saltwater – namely our seas and oceans – has long been thought of as a restorative. The earliest recorded work on different salts and how they are best used was published in China around 2700 BCE; the Greek physician Hippocrates was an advocate of seawater immersion to heal patients; and in the 1700s the English physician Richard Russell was a strong advocate for both the drinking of and submersion in sea water to treat glandular conditions. Sea bathing and sea air remain great healers of the general public and we can recreate a little of that magic at home with our own saltwater immersion.

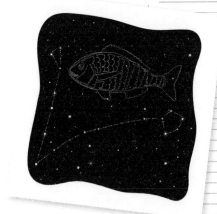

So this March let's bring the ocean into our homes no matter where we live, and indulge in a salt wash. For those of you with access to a bath, your task is merely to run it as hot as you like, light some candles, choose some music or sounds if they help you relax, or else enjoy the silence.

Homemade salt wash

100g / 3½ oz coarse sea salt or Himalayan salt
    (I like to use a mix of 80g coarse salt to
    20g pink Himalayan salt)
50g / 1¾ oz Epsom salt
1 tbsp bicarbonate of soda (baking soda)
Dried lavender flowers or peppermint leaves (I split a
    peppermint teabag, for ease)
5–10 drops of peppermint or lavender essential oil

Mix all of the ingredients together in a non-metallic bowl, and that's really all there is to it! You can use as much or as little as you need in the bath; just add to running water and allow the salts and herbs to soothe your skin and muscles. They also make very pretty, cheap and easy presents if you save old condiment and jam jars, clean off the labels and add your own, especially if you do add pink salt for colour. You can even change the oils for different purposes; adding citrus oils and peel for an energizing soak, or rose oils and petals for an indulgent one.

Epsom salt is a naturally occurring salt, different to the table salt and sea salt we know and cook with. It's a compound of magnesium and sulfate, and is used by physiotherapists and athletes to help heal and soothe sore muscles and aching bodies.

If you don't have access to a bath, why not make a salt scrub you can use in the shower instead? Take a handful of salt flakes, place them in a bowl, and add melted coconut oil or sweet almond oil until they're almost covered. Then add a few drops of your favourite essential oil and gently stir the mix. Use it in the shower to gently massage and scrub your skin, but take care, as the oil will make the shower floor slippery – use a mat if you have one, or consider putting a towel down to keep yourself safe. Rinse off after you've finished and enjoy your soft, salt-washed skin.

In writing

My book choice for this month is a beautiful, intimate and intricate piece of non-fiction. **Secrets of a Devon Wood** is a nature journal by **Jo Brown**, documenting the small wonders of the wood behind her home in Devon, UK. The pages in the book are an exact replica of the journal she began in 2018, and the discoveries are presented in the order she found them, beginning in April. Each illustration is based on a photograph Jo took, and the result is a colourful, uplifting, bright and accessible guide to the nature she saw every day, complete with little snippets of information.

I chose it because it's one of the most beautiful and accessible nature books I've ever seen. Unlike many nature writers, Jo's work is based in her locale; there is no travel involved, no specialist equipment. Just keen observation and an innate curiosity and desire to learn, and the spirit of the book is exactly the kind of thing I hope to foster with this almanac. I loved it so much it inspired me to start drawing my own discoveries, and while I don't have even a hundredth of the talent Jo has, the act of finding or photographing something and then bringing it home to draw and muse upon added a lovely sense of peace and accomplishment to my nature rambles.

You can read through the guide cover to cover, or flick through and pick out the pictures that speak to you; it covers amphibians, reptiles, birds, lichens, fungi, plants, insects, arachnids and more. It's a gentle book, a real gift of a read, and, just like with this almanac, there is a section at the back where you can make your own drawings and observations.

Voices, past and present

A selkie, for those who don't know, is a kind of shapeshifter from Scottish mythology which can remove its seal skin on land and appear human for a time. It's said if you take the skin of a selkie and hide it away you can keep the selkie by your side, but if they ever find their skin again, they'll put it on and forget you, forget the life you led together, and return joyfully to the sea. There's something about the selkie, emerging from the cold grey seas to live under the sun for a while, that makes me think of March, and the shedding of old winter skin. We'll go back to the sea, because life is a circle, but for a while, beginning now, we'll have time under a warm sun.

Tame: A poem in three parts

1

To make a wild thing tame.
A calm voice and gentle motions. Don't reach out at first, but keep close by.

You can't hurry a wild thing, it's two steps forward and one step back; the wind might be wrong, the signs disturbing and you have to accept that. There are stars and retrogrades at play, cards to be dealt and deciphered. Consider the seasons. Just when you think you've done it, she will slip away beneath the waves and you'll need to begin again.

Patience is a virtue
is wearing thin
is perseverance.
Try, try again.

You have to be willing to wait, every day on the cliffs, sat downwind with a flask of tea and a packet of sandwiches to keep mind and body together. You must remember to take all your litter home with you, don't disturb the ground too much, leave no marks behind.

You have to get the wild thing used to you, you see.

Then, when the time's right, you make a shelter from the storm – it doesn't have to be a very good one – a safe harbour in your arms where waves can't batter the wild thing against rocks, and soon enough you'll have her eating from the palm of your hand and coming when you call, wild thing no more.

2

To hold a wild thing.
Know that she can live a long time dying, never noticing the collar being lovingly laid around her neck.

A chain is still a chain, whether it's iron or gold, but she will never think of that when you hold it up to the light and it shines.

The links seem so small and delicate from a distance.

If done right, a knife can be slid in almost painlessly. It's only really the first part that hurts; after that it's easy enough to keep pushing.

The skin will part with a curtsey, the fat will yield like water and then she's yours.
Eventually she won't even remember she once was something else.

Day by day, week by week, year by year you'll add twigs to a dam built where she stands. One day it will become a pyre you'll ask her to dance on. And dance she will, hands tied behind her back to a stake she now calls home.

While you tell her you love her and flick matches at her feet.

3

To be tame.

"Go fuck yourself," you say, but kindly; it isn't meant to be cruel, it's just how you talk to each other now.

You don't worry anymore when she leaves and walks with her hands bunched up in fists that wouldn't make space for your thick fingers if you went after her. She'll come home eventually; you put butter on her paws, so to speak. Hands/paws/flippers, what difference does it make?

And sometimes vinegar is more useful than honey, especially with a woman who has too much salt in her water, even now.

But the thing you'll never understand, is that when you tire of her – and you will – you can't just set her free. You can't rewild a tamed thing.

You can't call a wild thing from the sea, take her skin and lock it away, and expect her to know what to do with it when you hand it back.

Louisa Adjoa Parker is not a winter person. She confesses while we talk that she would cheerfully hibernate until the sun came back. Now a writer and diversity consultant, Louisa has spent most of her life living in the southwest of England. She is a sea person – like me, someone who is both energized and soothed by the water – and is in fact writing a coastal memoir, examining her life and growing up with the sea, when we speak. As we talk about being near the water, her voice ebbs and flows like the tide; rising enthusiasm followed by gentle, sighing gratitude for the peace and beauty it gives her. It's enough to make me press my face against the corner of my window. I'm lucky; I can see the sea from here. It's grey today, blending with the sky beyond.

Despite Louisa's deep, abiding love for the sea, and the fact she lives only half an hour away from the coast, she doesn't get to visit as much as she'd like. I've been thinking a lot about selkies lately, and Louisa's wistfulness as she tells me she must go back soon reminds me of their stories, of women lured away from the saltwater homes they love and trapped on land, their seal skins locked in chests to keep them from returning to the water. Today it isn't fishermen hungry for wives that keep selkie women from the ocean, but modern life obligations instead. We're landlocked by circumstance.

For Louisa, part of the challenge of spending time in nature, especially as an adult, isn't just tied to her everyday life, but to her very real skin. Louisa is mixed heritage, and knows that her skin colour means she stands out among the white-skinned, brisk, wellies-and-wax-jacket stalwarts of British countryside we most associate with nature lovers. She tells me she often feels invasive when entering new green spaces; to engage with nature she has to deal with the fear that she won't be accepted and that it's not a place for her. We discuss how British nature writing or media isn't very diverse, but how tourism – impact on the climate and other ecological issues aside – is perhaps making it easier for people of colour to go to the countryside, and be in nature without being questioned. Afterwards, when I'm listening back to our talk, I think how terrible it is that a huge swathe of British society only gets a day pass to the world they live in, and how much that has to change.

We talk about how the climate disaster is terrifying, but also how it's making people realize nature is right there, outside, and if they don't move to see it now then they might miss the chance. Louisa, like a growing number of women, is starting to feel the call of the outdoors again, and wants to return to it. She is gleeful when she tells me about her childhood and teen years, leaving the house to join packs of other teenagers outside away from prying adult eyes, hiding in bluebell woods to smoke cigarettes and kiss boys. We talk about how it seems easier when you're a child to find a place in the outdoors, as if being a child makes you a little bit more feral, a little bit more animal, enabling you to vanish into the undergrowth, to climb trees, to dip your feet in frogspawn-y ponds without being afraid it's not for you. When you're a child, you know it's yours.

Louisa explains there have been times when she's struggled with anxiety, that back then she didn't know it was anxiety, and how, in the initial absence of medical help, she developed her own coping mechanisms using nature and the outdoors to ground her. "I'd go down to this beach, Monmouth Beach, which is really wild... black cliffs, grey clay with fossils in, trees in the distance, the shingle beach with a little bit of sand and lots of grey pebbles. I'd go down there on my own if I could, and basically just walk, and that would help me to feel like I could make sense of myself. Almost like a grounding thing for me, I think."

Her love and gratitude for it coats every word; she talks as if she's there right now – breathing salt air, face turned to a cloud-smeared sun – not recounting a memory from years before. Being there, she says, helped her to understand her place in the world and put her problems into perspective. It balanced her. It's something she craves more and more. That balance. That sense of rightness.

"When I'm with my oldest friends, when we get together and walk on a beach, it feels timeless. We've been doing that together for thirty years. And it feels like some things change, but something about being by the sea is timeless and doesn't change. We're all just here for the blink of an eye, really, but the sea and the landscape – that's been here for thousands of years and it will be here long after we're not, and there's something about that that just makes you feel good." For some, the vast unknown of the sea is terrifying, but for people like Louisa and me, that's part of the lure. It's a part of nature we know we belong to, and belongs to us; beneath our skins, there's fur and flippers.

March

In your hands

April

Regarding April

It's not accurate to say that April is the month everything gets started in the outside world, but it is the month where even the most oblivious person notices the changes that are happening around them, day by day.

April is a flirty month. It's all coy glances and lovingly padded nests and aerial displays of courtship. The migrating birds that herald summer in the UK are starting to arrive: swifts, martins and swallows. The nightingale is back, and so is the cuckoo, though both are sadly on the Red List due to drastic declines over the past 40 years. It doesn't help the cuckoo's case that it doesn't have the good PR of the nightingale – while the latter is adored for its song and its place in fairy tales, the former is reviled for its parasitic nesting habits. I suppose it's hard to sympathize with a bird that deliberately lays its eggs in other birds' nests so they'll do the drudge work of raising the chick, not to mention the way said chick will out-and-out murder its "siblings" so it can dominate its adoptive parents'

attention. But I don't think you get to frown upon the dodgy habits of the cuckoo if you're a human being, so the less said about it the better.

What else?

In the western US, rufous hummingbirds and black-chinned hummingbirds are starting to return from their winter holidays to the south (lucky west-coast residents have one year-round hummingbird, Anna's hummingbird). The western tanager will be arriving back for their breeding season, as will the tree swallow and the varied thrush, although you're only likely to see those in thick conifer woodland. Keep an eye out for various warblers and flycatchers too.

Also in the skies, bats will be waking from hibernation! There are 18 species of bat that live in the UK, 17 of them breed here, and over 40 make their home in the US. July's interview is with someone who spends a huge part of her summer counting them.

Some British woods (and in some US ones, where they are an invasive species) should still be full of bluebells, so if you didn't manage to see any last month, here's another chance. One word of caution: it's become popular for people to surround themselves with bluebells for photos, which inevitably means wading into the thick of them. But it actually takes bluebells several years to establish themselves. Please don't stand on them or damage them in any way. Not only are they protected, but you're harming something that will take a long time to recover, if at all, all for a few likes on social media. Post a photo of a kitten instead, and leave the bluebells alone.

In the ponds, the frogspawn and toadspawn have hatched and the water will be riddled with tadpoles that have survived so far. Some of it might even be newt spawn – if it develops front legs first, it's a smooth newt; back legs, a frog, though you'll have to wait a while to see that happen.

In the UK, badger cubs will be out of the sett and playing nearby, though I'd advise against going to look, as their parents are ferociously protective. And in the US, skunk kits are beginning to be born. They'll stay in their dens with their mothers until they're around six weeks old, so don't expect to see any just yet.

By now you should be feeling quite adventurous and regularly venturing out of your own sett or den, whether literally or digitally. Hopefully you've spent the past three months gently, and then maybe less gently, introducing yourself to whatever natural spaces you've found; you have been working on bringing nature into your home and routine, and you're starting to feel confident that there is a place for you in the natural world. I'm hopeful that you're starting to fall, or fall back, in love with the outside world and that love is growing on its own terms as you find the best way for you to be in it. But it's all right if you're not quite there yet. We still have eight months of the year left. Really, we're just getting started.

In the skies

April is a busy month in the skies.

Firstly, it offers not one but **two new moons**. Occurring on the very first and last days of the month, at **06:24 GMT on the 1st** and at **20:28 GMT on the 30th,** the second new moon is known as a black moon.

April's full moon is most commonly called the **Pink Moon**, named because April is the month when pink wild ground phlox first appears after winter. It's sometimes known as the **Fish Moon, Egg Moon** or **Sprouting Grass Moon** – for the eggs laid by birds after winter, for the return of greenery and grass, and for the fish that return to the rivers to spawn. **April's full moon occurs at 18:55 GMT on the 16th**, sandwiched between the two new moons.

April also gifts us with our second regular meteor shower of the year. Over the night and morning of **22–23 April, if the skies are clear we'll see the Lyrids.** It's a quieter shower than the Quadrantids in January, with a peak of 20 meteors per hour. Use Star Walk to find the constellation Lyra and watch from there for the best chance of seeing them.

And finally, the **first solar eclipse of the year will happen on the 30th**. It's just a partial, and will only be visible in South America and the southeast Pacific Ocean, but if you find yourself there, and have the appropriate eye equipment or a pinhole viewer, you might get to see it.

In the soil

PLANTS YOU CAN SOW THIS MONTH: Tomatoes, strawberries, peppers, peas, spinach, carrots, basil, chives, rosemary, mint. If you started spring onions (scallions) last month and are ready to move your shoots into bigger pots, why not start more seeds to keep a steady crop available? (It's called a succession crop.)

Basil is a fast, happy grower, and will grow leaves to replace any you pick so long as you don't strip a whole plant. To keep my supply plentiful and allow the plants time to recover in between harvests, I sow multiple seeds in a single 25cm plastic pot on my kitchen windowsill, planting four or five seeds at least 2 inches away from the edge of the pot, and each other. Basil likes a lot of sun, so keep that in mind – I keep it beside my tomatoes. It's also best not to let it grow too tall; trimming it after it gets above 6 inches will help keep it bushy and productive.

Rosemary likes an alkaline soil. You don't necessarily need to get a separate potting mix for it; you can get agricultural lime from garden centres and mix a teaspoon of that into your potting soil. You harvest it in a similar way to basil, just taking a few sprigs at a time from different plants, so again I grow multiple plants in one pot – three in a 25cm pot. It also likes warmth and sun, and prefers not to be watered very often – I keep mine under a cloche and allow it to get its moisture from condensation, but misting it once a day when it's very warm will work too.

Chives will also replace shoots you've harvested from each plant so long as you don't take too many, so again, plant three or four in a 25cm container and you can begin cutting from them around 30 days after planting if they're taller than 15cm. They, like basil and rosemary, will grow all year round indoors, providing they have enough light, but not too much.

Mint is a sprawling plant and needs room to grow, so maybe veto this one if space is limited. It's also difficult to raise from seed, so it's OK to cheat with this one and buy an existing plant, or ask if you can take cuttings if you know someone who has one. If you have room, then sow one or two seeds (no more) in a pot no smaller than 25cm. Harvest a few leaves at a time.

Check List:

- ☐
- ☐
- ☐
- ☐
- ☐
- ☐
- ☐
- ☐

MAINTENANCE THIS MONTH: Move anything that's grown tall enough into new pots. Tomatoes, chillies and strawberries will need to be one plant per pot, but peas can be two per pot, at opposite sides, provided the pot is at least 30cm wide. Spring onions (scallions) can be sown very close together, just give them an inch or two around each other and the sides of the pot.

HARVESTING THIS MONTH: It's possible you'll be able to harvest the first of your microgreens for an early salad! Once they get to 2 inches tall, you can start snipping. Otherwise, hold fire. It's also possible early radishes will be available, and baby leaf spinach, too.

In season

April is the start of the two months known to market gardeners as the Hungry Gap, as it's the time of year when the least fresh fruit and vegetables are available to harvest. It's significantly leaner in the fruit world, where only rhubarb, bananas and kiwi fruit are readily in season, but things are a little cheerier in the vegetable world.

Asparagus has come into season, along with **broccoli, Jersey Royal new potatoes**, **purple sprouting broccoli, radishes**, **spinach** and **spring onions (scallions)**.

This month's recipe is deceptively simple, but tastes exactly like the beginning of spring. April might be sparse for fresh produce, but it's also the best month for **Jersey Royal new potatoes**, and so takes advantage of them, and the first spring onions. Jersey Royals have a sweetish, nutty flavor and are a stalwart of the finest potato salads, but I think we can do better than drowning them in mayonnaise (this time, at least) and allow them to be the star of the show. Let me introduce you to smashed Jersey Royals with garlic, spring onions and olive oil. You can eat them as an accompaniment or side dish, or you could do as I do, and just eat them as a filling lunch or light tea. The very bravest of you could even forage your own wild garlic, as it's also in season, and if you started growing spring onions back in February, you might find the first of them are ready to eat!

Smashed Jersey Royals

Ingredients

Jersey Royal potatoes - as many as you want to eat!

1 garlic clove / 5 or 6 leaves of washed wild garlic

A glug of the nicest extra virgin olive oil you have

A couple of spring onions (scallions)

Black coarse pepper

Sea salt

Method

1. Wash the potatoes thoroughly, but don't peel them. Place them in a pan of cold, generously salted water and bring to the boil. Then simmer for 15-20 minutes, until a knife goes easily into them but they still have their shape. Drain them, but keep the pan aside (and warm).

2. If using garlic cloves: Add a small amount of the olive oil to the pan and heat it, then crush and add the garlic. Let it lightly sauté, but not brown. When soft, remove from the heat and add the potatoes and another glug of olive oil to the pan. Using a rolling pin or similar, smash the potatoes up - don't mash them, just rough them up a bit. Serve with sliced spring onion (scallion) and a sprinkle of black pepper and a touch of salt. If you have a cut lemon handy, a squeeze of lemon juice will brighten it too.

If using wild garlic: Add the potatoes to the still-warm pan and the olive oil and swirl it all around. Using a rolling pin or similar, smash the potatoes up - don't mash them, just rough them up a bit. Tear and toss the wild garlic leaves in. Serve as above with sliced spring onion, salt and a sprinkle of black pepper, and a squeeze of lemon juice if you like.

In the home

The outdoor world is getting busy as everything becomes about homes and nests! So your job this month is to help make your home a place that supports nature, and you can do that in a few different ways.

The first is to find some way to feed the local birdlife. Even the busiest city has a healthy population of birds, and at this time of year adult birds are expending an enormous amount of energy on caring for their new hatchlings, or finishing their nests, and they could really use your help. If you have a balcony, window or garden, find some way to set up a feeding station. It could be a hanging cage, a bird table, or just nuts and seeds scattered along a windowsill. It might take a little while to attract them, but once they realize there is a steady supply of food available, they'll keep coming back. Keep an eye out for which birds come, and use the Internet to adjust your offerings to best suit their diet. Bread is never the right option, but nuts, seeds, mealworms, fat balls, etc. are all welcome!

One word of note is that the RSPB recommends that if you begin feeding birds, you should keep it up all year round, so only start feeding them if you feel you can commit to it. It is a special kind of joy to see birds so close, but if you don't think you can sustain it, or if you're worried about attracting other animals/birds that you would welcome less, then maybe idea number two is for you.

Idea number two concerns our pollinators! If you have a balcony, garden, or safe, wide windowsill, plant a pot or bed of butterfly- and bee-attracting flowers, such as lavender, chives, saxifraga Peter Pan, aubretia and wall flowers, which are all appealing to pollinators. If you have enough space, consider adding a bee hotel, or making one out of bamboo canes.

Number three – if you have a garden, think about how navigable it is for wildlife. Do you have any frequent visitors you're aware of? Maybe you could make things easier for them to pass through, cut holes in fences, add ramps, or even a small pond (if you're feeling very brave, and you own your home or have the landlord's permission). If not, you can put down small dishes of water for them – animals need clean, fresh water too.

Doing these things will both support the wildlife local to you and bring it a little closer to your home, where you can watch it thrive knowing you're doing something to help.

In your phone

Rather than recommend a new app this month, I'm going to ask you to use one you already have, and probably already use a lot! Now spring is officially here, and the natural world is visibly busy, April is a great time to start recording the nature you see when you're out and about in the world, with your camera.

Whether it's colours that are vibrant and striking, flowers and leaves that are especially beautiful to you, patterns in the clouds, or glimpses of birds, insects or other wildlife, take a photo of them to help you remember the moment. This is something I do a lot through spring and summer, hoarding the photos for dark rainy days when it feels like it'll never stop being gloomy. I scroll back and find the proof that it will stop, that the circle of life will keep turning and everything will be lovely again.

Hopefully you've been using the "In your hands" section of the almanac to document your thoughts and feelings through the first months of the year, but why not consider printing out some of your photos and adding those to it, too?

In caring for yourself

To celebrate the arrival of spring we're going to slough off our winter skin – literally, with a homemade sugar scrub.

Homemade sugar scrub

4 tbsp brown sugar

4 tbsp coconut oil

¼ tbsp sweet almond oil

¼ tbsp lemon juice

4–6 drops of your favourite essential oil

Simply mix all of the ingredients together in a bowl, and then use in the shower. It's really that simple! You can make it a little in advance and keep it in the fridge, or just as and when you want it. In the fridge it will stay fresh for a week, at least.

In writing

The Bees by **Laline Paull** is my choice for April, and I think it's safe to say that if you're not already familiar with it then it's like nothing you've ever read before.

It's narrated by Flora 717, a honeybee. And what follows is the story of Flora's fight for autonomy and self-determination in an environment that demands she conform and do her duty or be killed. From the very beginning, Flora is an outlier, and is saved from execution by the Queen, whom she goes on to serve. But Flora is not very good at following the hive's diktat: Accept, Obey, Serve, and after the Queen's potent pheromones – which are supposed to ensure the hive follows her orders – lose their power, Flora's impulses lead her into the gravest of danger, with the highest possible rewards.

The Bees is a complex look at the realities of bee life – Laline Paull began to write the novel after reading a book about the creatures and realizing how complex, hard and unforgiving the lives of female bees are. The drones do nothing except wait for the chance to mate with the Queen (even though it will kill them) while the female honeybees are the foragers, guards, cleaning crew, builders, food preparers, nurses and handmaidens to the larvae and Queen, AND are expected to feed and clean up after the drones too!

It also looks at the politics of what it is to be female and to occupy a space with no hope of change or escape, simply because of the way you were born.

Unless, of course, you are like Flora 717 and take control of your own destiny, defying the expectations and demands set upon you and breaking free from the confines of the hive. The hive is important, and so is community, but it's just as important to have a sense of self and to try to follow your heart. It's strange to live a story through the eyes of a bee, and it's sometimes uncomfortable and bleak too, but it's also a fascinating look inside the hive, one of nature's most intricate and savage communities. And it's a chance for us to think about the roles we occupy in our own hives, and whether they serve us as much as we serve them. After all, we're not bees.

Voices, past and present

In the UK, April is when the skylarks start to breed, and when you're likely to see the jaw-dropping displays of male skylarks rising almost vertically up into the air and singing. It's possible for them to hover at heights of 1,000 feet before they finally begin to descend, their territory well and truly established. I was hoping to share a superstition or folktale about skylarks here, but they seem to be one of the rare birds where the reality of them is more compelling than any story, and I hope one day I'll get to see it for myself and understand why the sight of a skylark shooting into the sky is so awe-inspiring to so many, including some of history's most revered poets.

The most famous celebration of the skylark in literature is surely in Percy Bysshe Shelley's "To a Skylark", the beginning of which contains some of the most joyful nature verses ever written. The first three stanzas are my favourites:

Hail to thee, blithe Spirit!
Bird thou never wert,
That from heaven, or near it,
Pourest thy full heart
In profuse strains of unpremeditated art.

Higher still and higher
From the earth thou springest
Like a cloud of fire;
The blue deep thou wingest,
And singing still dost soar, and soaring ever singest

In the golden lightning
Of the sunken sun,
O'er which clouds are bright'ning,
Thou dost float and run,
Like an unbodied joy whose race is just begun.

When I first approached acclaimed novelist and screenwriter Catherine Johnson to ask her about her relationship with nature, the plan was that we'd drive out to Rye and chat while we watched skylarks rising up into the air. I've never seen a skylark, but Catherine loves them, loves the way they shoot heavenwards, loves the sound of their song. They make her think of her mother, and how she loved to watch them when she was a child, living in north Wales. Catherine went on annual holidays back to her mother's village throughout her childhood, though she never saw a skylark there; chemicals used on fields put paid to their appearance by the time she started going.

The part of Wales her mother was raised in was so rural that her grandmother, the main reason holidays were taken there, didn't have electricity – instead, after dark, rush tapers would be lit, and she still has one of the holders used for the job. The image lends itself completely to the way Catherine got to experience the kind of bucolic, idyllic summer holidays that would have Enid Blyton furiously scribbling down notes: cutting peat for the fires, wandering the countryside alone for hours, heading up to the "big house" to lurk around the stables, befriending the grooms and helping out in exchange for the occasional chance to ride a horse. The local sheep-herding ponies needed riding too, and Catherine was a regular volunteer.

Catherine was – and still is – horse mad. Back home in London after the holidays were over, she was a part of the City's surprising (to me, at least) and thriving horse and pony scene; she learned to drive a horse from the draymen who worked for Hanbury brewery.

"There were loads of stables in London. In the arches behind Hackney Town Hall, behind the baker in Broadway Market. In Tower Hamlets. Spitalfields City Farm, Kentish Town City Farm. I had a permit to ride on Hampstead Heath. You could easily be a horse girl in the heart of London."

Now living in East Sussex, she rides whenever she can, still spending hours at the stables, mucking out horses, feeding them and just being near them. She likes the way they smell: "grassy and biscuity and warm. They just smell *good*."

We talk about how even horse poo smells good; how compared to the stools of other animals it smells almost clean, and definitely wholesome, quintessentially something from the countryside, something natural.

Catherine moved to East Sussex with her then-husband, and at first had very little time with her beloved horses, something she missed. Slowly, she began making connections and getting back into riding. At the same time, her marriage was falling apart, and she credits horses as being one of the things that kept her strong throughout the process of divorce, and dividing up a life into two.

"When you're on a horse, you can only really think about what's happening then. You can't let yourself get caught up in your own head: you have to focus on the horse, and the path; you have to be aware of what's around you, what's ahead of you, because it's your job to keep you and the horse safe. So it's a break from your own thoughts."

As well as the peace of mind it brings by forcing her to be present, she also appreciates how being around horses and spending time in their environment brings her closer to wildlife and plants, and offers other, tastier opportunities. A few days before I typed this up, Catherine messaged me to say she was bringing me a whole bunch of field mushrooms she'd found in one of the fields, and I used them that night to make mushroom fried rice for my dinner. She also found a bunch of wild sloes, and harvested some to make gin.

"On horseback you're higher off the ground, so you see things from literally a different perspective. You notice the shapes of hills, you notice the trees around you, and you see early on when they start to change. Being higher up also means you look up; I see buzzards, sparrowhawks, swallows and pheasants. And for some reason horses don't spook wild animals in the same way humans do, so I get to see glimpses of wildlife that I might not if I was just walking. Being on horseback takes me off the beaten track."

The best thing she's seen is skylarks. Finally, after a lifetime looking for them in Wales, she found them right here, at home.

"I feel my heart lift when they do."

April

In your hands

May

Regarding May

May holds such a special place in the collective heart of the UK, and not just because it has two Bank Holidays (or Extra Going Outside Days, as you might like to think of them now). If April was a flirt, then May is a bawd, not a hint of subtlety, with all possible plumage and blooms on show, begging you to come and join in the fun. May is a month of abundant fecundity, rich in colour and fragrance. Whatever timidness had been in the natural world before, it's gone now and everything is a festival. May is about celebration and fertility and daring. So be daring this month. Travel a little further, tread the paths a little less well known.

If you're housebound, and financially able, order yourself some vibrant flowers, or demand someone who loves you does. Invite colour inside, and revel in it. Split bouquets into a few stems and dot them everywhere. Surround yourself.

This is the time of year when wild garlic grows rampant, and I'd urge you to find some and cook with it, if you can, though take care to be sure it is wild garlic. Check, check again and if possible get someone else to check too, any time you're foraging wild food to eat. There are often courses available; it's worth looking them up if foraging is something that appeals to you. If you do start to forage, don't take anything that is protected, endangered or vulnerable, be sure the land and the plants are not privately owned, never take roots or do anything that would stop them growing back, only ever take a little from places where there is a plentiful supply, and always leave enough for the wildlife that needs it to survive. Foragers in the US will need to check state and municipal law before foraging as laws on what can and can't be taken vary vastly, and also be aware that spraying of all plants with chemicals to keep weeds in check is much more commonplace, especially along the sides of roads and near areas with houses or services (though it's sadly on the rise in the UK, so be aware here too, and also if you're foraging near farmland). If the area looks remotely upkept, avoid taking anything.

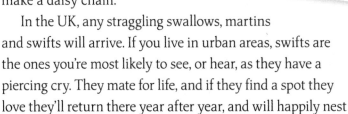

Trees will be heavy with blossom; hawthorn, crabapple and rowan all flower in May. In the US the dogwoods will be blooming, as will the black hawthorn. Red clover, oxeye daisies and buttercups will poke through the grass. No one is ever too old or too cool to make a daisy chain.

In the UK, any straggling swallows, martins and swifts will arrive. If you live in urban areas, swifts are the ones you're most likely to see, or hear, as they have a piercing cry. They mate for life, and if they find a spot they love they'll return there year after year, and will happily nest under the eaves of roofs. Swifts are related to hummingbirds, despite bearing a resemblance to martins and swallows. Sadly, like a lot of British and British-visiting birds, their numbers are declining too.

In the US, mid-May is the height of hummingbird breeding season, and the males can be quite loud while they compete for the females, who are off building impossibly tiny nests. Keep an eye out for them in your gardens if you know there are populations nearby – the young hatch roughly fourteen days after laying and fledge just three weeks later.

If you live in the west of Britain, near a river, May offers a chance to see sea trout swimming upstream to spawn. Other river and pond watchers might see the first of the mallard ducklings or moorhen chicks. If you live near the countryside or can get to a city farm, then take advantage of lambing season; it's always lovely to watch fearless, joyful lambs gamboling and jumping around. They're so sweet and silly, you can't help feeling lifted by them.

If sweet and joyful isn't quite your cup of tea, then maybe snakes will be? Once it begins to get reliably warm, May is a good time to spot basking grass snakes, which are completely harmless to humans. They like wetlands best of all, and can often be found near ponds and lakes; they're excellent swimmers. We have two other species of snake in the UK: the smooth snake, which is very rare and only found at a few heathland sites, and the adder, our only venomous snake. Adders emerge from hibernation earlier than the grass snake, usually in late March, and live in woodlands and heathland.

They are exceedingly shy, and will flee if they hear you coming. However, if you do manage to surprise one, it may bite, and you'll need to seek immediate medical attention.

In the US, you're most likely to come across the common garter snake, but I would strongly advise you to stay away from all snakes you encounter in the wild, as North America is home to 21 species of venomous snake, including the relatively common Western rattlesnake. To be safe, look instead for skinks and lizards, like the sagebrush lizard in shrubland, the western fence lizard in western states, and the western skink through most of the Pacific Northwest. On the east coast, you could also spot the American blue-tailed skink, also known as the five-lined skink. If you must go looking for snakes, remember to move carefully, watch where you tread, and to keep a safe and respectful distance from anything you do come across. That goes for UK readers too.

The weather is reliably warm enough to start wearing a jacket if you're bold enough to cast your clout before May is out, but if you are, please remember to wear sunscreen if your skin is bared.

In the skies

Not to be outdone by last month's celestial bonanza, May has quite the full calendar too.

The night of the 6th and early morning of the 7th gives us the Eta Aquariids shower – and assuming the skies are clear the waxing moon will set early enough for us to see some of the 30 or so meteors we can expect in the northern hemisphere, while observers in the south can see up to 60! As the name indicates, the constellation Aquarius is the one to watch for the best chance.

The full moon, the Flower Moon, occurs at 04:14 GMT on the 16th, and also hails the first full lunar eclipse of the year. A lunar eclipse occurs when the moon travels through the Earth's umbra – or shadow – which blocks the light of the sun from reaching it. The lack of direct light causes the moon to appear red – which is why lunar-eclipsed moons are called blood moons. It will be visible throughout all of North America and parts of western Europe, including the UK, as the moon sets, at 5:10am.

Our new moon is at 11:30 GMT on the 30th.

In the soil

PLANTS YOU CAN SOW THIS MONTH: Peas, spinach, carrots, basil, chives, rosemary, mint.

MAINTENANCE THIS MONTH: Move anything tall enough into its own pot.

Keep an eye on your herbs and thin those back to keep healthy new growth. You can infuse the leaves in oil, or even freeze them in oil in ice-cube trays to store them if you can't immediately use them.

If you're growing **vine tomatoes**, you'll need to pinch out the little side shoots that grow out of the main leaf joins, as they will sap valuable energy from the plant. If you're growing bush varieties like Tiny Tims, no extra pruning is needed (though I do sometimes pinch out the side shoots just to reduce the foliage).

On your **chillies**, begin trimming the tops once they get to around six inches high to keep the plant bushy instead of tall. Also pinch off any early flowers; they'll sap the plants' energy. Flowers in May can be safely removed.

Move your **peas** and **strawberries** outdoors if you can, when the last of the frosts have definitely passed. The peas will need staking to help keep them steady as they grow. I use bamboo canes and jute string to carefully tie mine to the stakes. While peas and strawberries (along with tomatoes and chillies) are self-pollinating, strawberries will benefit from the attention and help of pollinators, so if you can't put

Check List:

- [ ]
- [ ]
- [ ]
- [ ]
- [ ]
- [ ]
- [ ]
- [ ]

them outside at all, be prepared to get a paintbrush and watch some videos on how to pollinate them.

One word of caution: if you're moving plants outside then you need to brush up on potential pests and start planning ways to combat them, including birds as far as berries are concerned! Birds love them as much as we do, so consider covering your growing fruits with a very fine mesh, to make sure birds can't get caught in it as they try to get your hard-grown fruits!

HARVESTING THIS MONTH: Basil, chives and rosemary if the plants are tall enough. Microgreens. Baby spinach leaves. Carrots. Spring onions (scallions). The first of the peas!

In season

The second month of the Hungry Gap, only **rhubarb**, **bananas** and **kiwi fruit** are in season. As far as vegetables go, the first of the **peas** should be appearing in shops, sweet and small at this time of year, best eaten popped straight out of the pod and into your mouth. **Asparagus, broccoli, carrots, lettuces, new potatoes, radishes, spinach** and **spring onions (scallions)** are also available.

One that might be new to you is marsh **samphire**, which also comes into season in May. Marsh samphire is an edible kind of succulent that tolerates salt water well, so often grows near the sea or estuaries. It's naturally very salty (obviously), so rinse it well before you eat it. It's lovely fried gently in butter (or your favourite dairy-free alternative) and must be eaten fresh, as it doesn't keep. Buy (or pick) only as you need.

Everyone has a banana bread recipe and everyone is complicit in the lie it is a bread, and not, in fact, a cake. Banana bread is a stalwart if you're like me and buy bananas fully intending to put them in a smoothie or slice them onto cereal, but somehow never get around to it. My recipe is a little more decadent than the usual, as I add a streusel topping. And as if that wasn't enough, if there's any banana bread left after three days, I start toasting it and smearing it with peanut butter, which is honestly the best way to eat it.

Streusel-topped banana bread

Ingredients

For the "bread":

3 large, ripe bananas

75ml / 2½fl oz odourless cooking oil

120g / 4¼ oz brown sugar

225g / 8oz plain (all-purpose) flour

1 tbsp baking powder

2 tsp cinnamon

½ tsp dried ginger

(You can also add pinches of mace, cloves or nutmeg, and feel free to bung in chocolate chips or chopped walnuts too)

For the streusel topping:

50g / 1¾ oz vegan butter (melted)

100g / 3½ oz brown sugar

25g / 1 oz plain (all-purpose) flour

Pinch of cinnamon

Method

1. Preheat the oven to 180°C / 350°F / gas mark 6 (use the heat to melt the butter for your streusel mix), and line or grease a loaf tin.

2. Mash the bananas with a fork, then mix with the oil and sugar. It will be lumpy and kind of gross – that's excellent.

3. In a separate bowl, mix together the flour, baking powder and spices.

4. By now your butter should have melted and you can make your streusel topping. Add the sugar, flour and cinnamon you set aside for the topping to a bowl, and pour the butter into it, stirring and mixing until it forms a loose, crumb-like texture.

5. Then it's time to add the wet cake mix to the dry ingredients. Using a wooden spoon, blend it all together, and pour into the greased / lined tin.

6. Spoon the streusel topping evenly over the top and bake. Check it after 20 minutes, covering it with foil if the topping is starting burn, then return to the oven for another 15–20 minutes, or until a skewer can pierce it cleanly. Once it does, gently put on a rack to cool. Try to wait for it to cool a little bit before you eat it.

In the home

Following on from March's spring cleaning, this month I'd like to share with you a couple of "recipes" for cleaning products you can use in the home that don't contain chemical ingredients. They're not antibacterial and are unlikely to kill germs as effectively as traditional cleaners, so bear that in mind, but they can be used as an alternative to traditional bleach and toilet cleaners if you can do so safely, and won't have a toxic impact on the environment.

Vodka cleaning spray

50ml / 3 tbsp vodka (cheap own brand is fine!)

30ml / 1fl oz / 2 tbsp Castile soap, or liquid soap (Ecover washing-up liquid is a good substitute for this)

300ml / 10½fl oz water

Essentials oils of your choice

A clean spray bottle (the kind used to mist plants, or thoroughly cleaned recycled ones that previously contained household cleaning products)

Add all of the ingredients to your bottle (using as much or as little essential oil as you like) and give it a gentle shake or two to mix it up. This spray can be used on most bathroom and kitchen surfaces, and on mirrors, though please be careful on wood or covered MDF or particle board.

Toilet fizzers

These are cute just to chuck down the toilet in between more thorough cleanings. They act a little like bath bombs, reacting with the water and gently fizzing, releasing sweet essential oils into the air. You will need a silicone ice-cube tray for this, and a non-metal spoon or spatula.

In a non-metallic bowl, mix together 250g / 9oz of bicarbonate of soda (baking soda) and 40g / 1½oz of citric acid. For the next part, you need to act very quickly, as adding liquid will begin the chemical reaction and you don't want that yet. Drop by drop, add 5–10 drops of an essential oil of your choice (tea tree and lavender are my favourites for this) and quickly mix them into the bicarb / citric acid blend. Using a spray bottle, add one or two fine sprays of mist, again mixing quickly to keep the products from fizzing. When it's all blended, use your fingers or a spoon to press the mixture into the ice-cube tray, and leave for eight hours to set. They should set into hard little nuggets that fizz cheerfully when you pop them into the toilet bowl.

Cleaning cloths

These are so super easy it's almost a cheat to include them, but the basics of it are any clothes you've got that are torn or stained, and can't be recycled or refurbished, can still have another life as cleaning cloths! Simply cut them into squares and store them away to use on mirrors, furniture, kitchen surfaces or even as dishrags. Then throw them in the washing machine with your clothes and use them again and again. One thing to be aware of is that while all clothes shed microfibres, cut fabrics will shed a little more, so if you have a Guppyfriend bag (a branded device that catches fibres before they can get into the water supply) or similar, then please use it!

In your phone

This month, as we begin to venture outside in earnest, I'd like you to find an app that you can use to help identify plants. I personally favour **LeafSnap**, as I've been using it for a while, but there are a variety out there – PlantSnap, FlowerChecker, iNaturalist, NatureGate – so my advice would be to explore the options; some are free, others contain adverts, some give instant results, others use human identification so can take longer. With most of them, all you need to do is take a clear, close-up photo of any plants you come across that you don't recognize or know, upload it, and wait for the results. It's especially useful if you, like me, are looking for hawthorn blossom for your May Day table, and aren't sure if what you're staring at is hawthorn, cherry blossom, Mexican orange blossom, or something else entirely! It's a fun, fast and easily accessible way to get to know the nature around you.

In caring for yourself

May Day is when the May Queen is crowned, and so this year I invite you to crown yourself, with your own flower crown. Ideal for wearing when you're out and about in nature, or in your garden, or simply sitting at home painting your nails. Embrace your inner May Queen – it couldn't be simpler!

To make your crown, you will need:

Moss-covered florist's wire, enough to wrap around the circumference of your head (or a suitable substitute if wire isn't available; you could try weaving thin willow or hazel sticks into a crown, or buy a pre-made headband)

Green florist's tape

Secateurs or sharp scissors

Fresh or plastic flowers and leaves of your choosing, depending on how long you want your crown to last (if using fresh make sure they get a good drink of water for at least a couple of hours before you use them)

Wrap the moss-covered wire / woven sticks around your head where you want your crown to sit, and add an extra inch to the measurement (to allow for the extra bulk of the flowers and to have room to tie it together). Twist the ends together and seal with the florist's tape. This is your crown base.

Using the green florist's tape, sort your flowers and leaves into small bundles and begin attaching the bunches to the crown base by laying the stems flat against the wire and taping them to it. When you come to add the next bundle, use them to cover the tape, and so on, as you work your way around, making sure to fill any the gaps with foliage and blooms, and to cover the join of the crown.

And there you have it. It's even more special if you use hawthorn blossom, which can traditionally only be gathered and brought inside on May Day, though please

be sure to ask the permission of the tree before you cut any blossoms away, lest you incur the wrath of the Fairy Queen (and only take a few, lest you disrupt the bees and other pollinators who have a job to do and an ecosystem to maintain!).

In writing

May's book is **Elizabeth-Jane Burnett's *The Grassling*,**
and it is, more than anything, a book about soil. It's a book
about roots, and belonging, and having that one place that
is truly your home, that place you feel an inescapable
connection to in your bones.

For generations Burnett's father's family have farmed in
Devon (her mother is Kenyan and so she engages with the
land from both a Devonian and Kenyan perspective), and the
book is a homage to her life there, and how she starts to
rediscover the land as her father is dying. She walks and
swims the places she's known since childhood, thinking
about the cycle of life and death and what it means, and how
the land we grow up on has a part to play in who we are.

Her experience as a poet shows in every word; the
language sometimes as lyrical and flowing as the water,
sometimes as barren and sparse as an empty field. She muses
on the connectedness of nature, and how we've changed
from working with it to making it work for us. All this, and in
the background is the creeping sense of grief because a
season of her life is ending, and there will be only change
coming. The earth beneath her feet is shifting, and to keep
growing she'll have to shift with it.

I read the last chapter outside, the fingers of my left hand
pressed into the soil. I wanted to be connected as it ended,
before I began again.

Voices, past and present

Until a few years ago I had never heard of Jack in the Green. I knew the May Bank Holiday was special in the folk calendar of the UK – Morris dancing, maypoles, May Queens – but I'd never come across the wholly pagan celebration that is Jack. And then I moved to Hastings in East Sussex and found myself taking part in a four-day festival culminating in a sacrifice to release the spirit of summer!

For the uninitiated, Jack in the Green is a relatively new folk festival that grew out of an older tradition in the 17th century, beginning with milk maids carrying elaborate floral garlands in May Day parades to tempt crowds into throwing coins for their favourites. It's believed the size and intricacy of garlands grew as they sought to compete with each other for the most coins, and that at some point other enterprising trade groups got involved, eager to raise funds, until it became the celebration recognized today when one guild, suspected to be the Sweeps Guild, eventually created one giant structure that would be worn as the guise of Jack, who had to die so summer could be born.

The Hastings Jack festival engulfs the entire town, particularly the Old Town. Ribbons and garlands are put up on front doors and businesses, pop-up stalls selling flower crowns appear. For the festival itself everyone dresses in their greenest finery, painting their faces to match, putting flowers and leaves in their hair. The Green Man is always a regular sight in Hastings; many houses have plaques fringed with oak leaves on or near their doors, and during Jack in the Green he is brought to life, the spirit of the town made manifest. For the four days of the festival Morris dancers can be heard and seen dancing in any spare corner of the town, and Jack's bogies – his wingmen/protectors/jailers, depending on which of them you believe – prowl the streets, adorning the faces of those who catch their eye with a green smear of Jack's magic. There is a lot of drinking, eating and music.

It culminates atop West Hill overlooking the sea. Jack, his bogies, the bogie-wives and a plethora of other characters make their way in a joyful procession up through the Old Town to the hill, where Jack is eventually sacrificed and his spirit released so summer will begin. Leaves are torn from his coat and everyone is allowed to keep one, just one, to give them luck for the coming year.

One person who doesn't need to tear leaves from the coat of a dying god for luck is May's Voice, author Alice Broadway. But though Alice has her own supply of luck-bearing foliage on tap, she is very much the indoor type, and cheerfully admits to having a strained relationship with the outside. Or at least she tries to. It seems the outside isn't quite willing to accept that, and it pulls out all the stops to woo her, including showering her with tokens of luck.

"I'd describe my relationship with nature as anxious avoidant," Alice tells me. "It's one of those things where I love nature and I know it does me good, but I'm also intimidated and a bit scared of it." Her main problem with nature is how it doesn't quite obey the rules, at least in the ways she finds easy to understand. Sometimes it does things in manageable, pretty ways, and she can freely appreciate and enjoy it, but then the flipside is when it also does weird, dark, messy, dirty and even creepy things, which she finds unnerving.

Despite that, she knows that being outside is a tonic for her, so she makes it as pleasant for herself as she can. Around two years ago she began a practice called The Outdoor Teacup, which she documents on Instagram. The idea behind it is that every day she takes a cup of tea and sits on her doorstep, facing her garden. Once she's taken a photo to record it, she puts her phone away and listens to the world outside, breathing in fresh air, taking that small moment of pause to check in with herself and enjoy being outside, albeit from the safety of the stoop.

Alice has noticed that she has this tendency to stick to the edges of outside where she can, her doorstep acting as a kind of liminal space between the outdoors and indoors, walking the line between grass and mud, and staying where it feels manageable and safe and easy for her to be outside. It frustrates her, though. "I'm drawn to nature," she says, "and in my dream life I'd be frolicking in forests and swimming in rivers and all of those things, but the reality is that it's really nice out, but I'm going to go inside now and calm down!"

She might be happiest in her home, but nature, it seems, will go to any lengths to tempt Alice out.

Even performing miracles. Because there is a patch of grass in Alice's garden where you are guaranteed to find four-leaf clovers.

"Our house is built on the grounds of an old munitions factory, and who knows what's in the soil, but I'm pretty sure it means our garden has some kind of weird magic. You'll find a four-leaf clover in our garden within seconds, so it's like having this tiny space that is a bit like those books you read when you're a kid: 'Here's where all the four-leafed clovers grow.'"

We're both charmed by the idea that it's a deliberate act by nature, compensating for something previously unlovely being there by growing something almost mythical in its place. It's exactly the kind of chaotic act of nature that would normally make Alice wary, if it wasn't for the fact that four-leaf clovers are impossibly charming and inherently wondrous.

"It feels like this tiny magical space, and there's probably an excellent scientific explanation for them being there, but we seem to have them and it's like they've been put there as an invitation, saying, 'Here's a reason for you to come outside; here's a reason for you to venture barefoot onto the grass; here's a reason you shouldn't tend to your grass too much so that lots of clover can grow.'"

What makes it even more curious is that it's a phenomenon peculiar to Alice's garden. Intrigued by the probability of having so many (and admitting she wasn't even sure she believed in them as a real thing, suspecting they might just be the trappings of tourist gift shops), she's scouted the local area and other gardens for them but hasn't spotted any. It's just in her garden, as if nature knows she needs a little more coaxing outside than maybe others do and is willing to show off the full force of its magic and wonder to do so.

Inspired by Alice's four-leaf clovers, I went out looking for my own. And I found one too, on my very first go. A little piece of luck, all of my own. A sign.

May

In your hands

June

Regarding June

June is the beginning of meteorological summer, and in my opinion is one of the nicest months of the year; warm enough to enjoy being outside, but not so warm that lethargy sets in. Its long, light nights are perfect for extra time outside, whether that's enjoying nature or a cold drink with friends.

The summer solstice that takes place toward the end of the month celebrates the longest day of the year – or, more accurately, the day the sun spends the most time above the horizon. The date of the solstice alters each year, because the orbit of the Earth is actually an ellipse, not a circle, so the orbital speed varies, meaning some years the solstice takes place as early as 20 June, and others as late as the 22nd.

If you've been keeping an eye on the old familiar places you found at the start of this journey, you'll probably be astonished at how much they've changed in a relatively short period of time. Even if you haven't, and you've been more of a nature-seeking nomad, you should still be able to spot the difference between photos you took in February, then April, and now, and on the webcams too. You'll see how the colours and textures have altered; things will be there that weren't there before; things that seemed so permanent will have vanished until next year. Nothing in nature is stagnant, nothing stays the same – even the trees that seem so solid and so stalwart are changing, blossoming, growing leaves, bearing fruit, housing insects, birds, squirrels. Everything keeps moving and that's how it stays alive. Lessons to learn.

If you're keen to continue foraging then keep an eye out for elderflowers this month; they can be used to make a delicious and delicate cordial. Look for wild roses, too – those old favourites from jars of petal perfume. Feel free to relive your youth by adding a bunch to a jar of water, putting it away and forgetting about it until you find a pot of filthy brown liquid a few months from now, or dry them for tea, or clean and add the petals to a salad. If you live near a shingle beach, sea kale is delicious right now, though it is protected by the Wildlife and Countryside Act 1981, so you must have permission from the landowner to take any. If permission is granted, the younger leaves are the nicest, and can be cooked (or not) as you would normal kale. Please be sure to leave enough for the plants to survive, though.

Animal-wise, May and June are excellent times to see badgers if you live near a sett, and you might be surprised to learn that you do! I wanted my whole life to see a badger, and finally managed it in early June, completely by accident. I was walking home and saw a creature I first thought was a very large cat lolloping ahead of me and it took me a moment to realize what it really was – finally, a badger, living around the corner from my flat all that time, in a fairly well-populated part of the town. I went back and watched them every night for a while, and I still go back often. Badgers tend to live in the same setts for generations, and use the same paths, so once you discover them you can return to those places with confidence. Their eyesight is terrible, but their hearing and sense of smell is excellent, so remain still and quiet and don't wear any strong scents – and above all leave them alone. Wild animals should stay wild; we're very bad for them, even when we mean well.

In the US, the first of the striped skunk kits will be out and about! Skunks are nocturnal, sleeping the day away to emerge at night to eat. They tend to keep within a few miles of their den, so if you do see one (or many) at this time of year it's likely to be local. Though they are very cute, it's best to stay back, both because of their famous scent-based defence system (if the tail goes up then it's time to calmly but swiftly leave) and because skunks, though usually docile, are also major carriers of the rabies virus. It's also possible you'll see mother Virginia opossums with their young. Like all marsupials, opossum joeys live in their mother's pouch for the first couple of months of their lives, feeding there before climbing onto her back, leaving her when they're around four and a half months old.

Young foxes will also be abroad too, and given the proliferation of them in towns and cities these days it's probably more challenging to not see one! They're very curious and playful, and a lot of fun to watch, so definitely seek out fox webcams if you can't get outside – *Springwatch* in the UK usually has one, and an Internet search will help. Foxes don't keep a permanent earth (a hole or hollow they use for sleep and to raise their cubs) year in and year out; they change, so the locations of cameras will as well.

Chicks will begin fledging too. As a general rule, if you see a fully feathered chick on the ground it's a fledgling; leave it alone (though stay near-ish if you can to deter predators like cats). The parents of a grounded chick will almost certainly be aware of where it is, and nearby. Please don't try to put it back in its nest as you might disturb other young (and interfering in nests is illegal, no matter the bird, and no matter your intentions). If you see a chick that has few or no feathers then it's a nestling and won't survive for long outside the nest, so take it to your nearest wildlife rescuer (search online and always call ahead).

As for insects, in the UK, look out for the European stag beetle, often referred to as *the* stag beetle. They're incredibly powerful-looking. And if you live near limestone areas, you might even get to see glowworms in grasses and hedges. In the US, watch out for the rugose stag beetle – it's very rare, but you never know your luck.

In the skies

Our **Strawberry Moon this month, occurring at 11:51 GMT on the 14th, is a supermoon**. To me, the moon is super every month, but what makes the moon *super* in the eyes of the rest of the world is that it is as close to the Earth as it can be, making the moon seem much bigger, and brighter, than usual.

This month also hosts the **summer solstice on 21 June, at precisely 9:14 GMT.** The solstice is a hugely important time in so many countries, cultures, religions and spiritual practices. In scientific terms, it marks the day of the year that sees the most daylight, and marks the point where the path of the sun in the sky is farthest north, as well as being the beginning of summer in the northern hemisphere. But in cultural terms, it has a history that goes back to ancient times; many stone circles and burial mounds, such as Maeshowe in Orkney and Bryn Celli Ddu on Anglesey, were built to align with the path of the sun during the solstice. In the Nordic countries and Baltic States, Midsummer's Day is a huge part of the calendar, and people celebrate with food, drink and fire ceremonies. In the UK, huge crowds gather at Stonehenge to see the sun rise through the stones, which were possibly arranged as a kind of calendar to mark the solstice.

June's new moon occurs at 02:52 GMT on the 29th of the month.

In the soil

PLANTS YOU CAN SOW THIS MONTH:
Basil, chives, rosemary, lettuce,
spinach, spring onions (scallions),
carrots, peas.

MAINTENANCE THIS MONTH: Keep an
eye on the foliage on your tomatoes
and judiciously trim it back if
necessary to expose the fruits to
sunlight – they won't ripen without it.
Use sharp scissors or a knife to cut
leaves away at the join. Do the same
for your basil as soon as you
notice flowers beginning (look in
the centre of the stems for
something that looks like lots of
small leaves growing all at
once), as once the basil flowers
the leaves will begin to be less
pungent and flavorful.

Also think about making
your own swift "compost tea".
Compost tea is the liquid
byproduct of using compost
bins to generate your own compost, but
you can easily make a version of your

Check List:

- [ ]
- [ ]
- [ ]
- [ ]
- [ ]
- [ ]
- [ ]
- [ ]

own. Add banana peels to a litre glass jar and fill with water, then seal. Leave it for a week and then use the water on your growing plants, for added nutrients.

Check everything for pests. With your indoor plants, make sure they're well ventilated.

Feed your tomatoes and chillies regularly with a liquid feed – once a week as soon as the first fruits start to form.

HARVESTING THIS MONTH: Basil, chives, rosemary, baby spinach, carrots, strawberries, peas, spring onions (scallions) – don't pull them straight out; loosen them up a day or two beforehand, microgreens, early tomatoes (if they're ripe; don't fret if they're not).

In season

It's berry season! The Hungry Gap is over and the first soft fruits of the year should be making an appearance now. **Bilberries, blueberries, cherries, gooseberries, greengages** and **strawberries** are all ripening with the increase in sunlight. Early **apricots** and **peaches** are available too, as well as **kiwi fruits**.

Things are becoming very ample in vegetable terms too: **artichokes, asparagus, aubergine (eggplant), beetroot (beets), broad (fava) beans, broccoli, carrots, courgettes (zucchini), fennel, green beans, kohlrabi, lettuces, mangetout (snow peas), new potatoes, pak choi, peas, radishes, runner beans, samphire, spinach, spring onions (scallions)** and early **tomatoes** are all in season. And anyone who missed **turnips** during the past three months will be relieved to know they are back too! Turnips are seasonally available nine months of the year, truly the MVP of the vegetable world.

Midsummer is the one day of the year you can rely on me to be up before sunrise, because I like to sit outside with a flask of tea and my breakfast and watch the sun come up. A couple of years ago, I became very fixated on the idea of making sunshine bread to eat as dawn broke. So I fiddled around with a soda bread recipe and came up with a vegan version, which I added caraway seeds to, and saffron for a golden colour. I also added dried edible marigold flowers too.

Midsummer soda bread

Ingredients

Vegan buttermilk (make this by adding 30ml / 1fl oz / 2 tbsp apple cider vinegar to 230ml / 7¾fl oz unsweetened soy milk). Make this before you begin weighing everything else out, as the bread mix comes together quickly and you'll need time for the buttermilk to curdle before you can add it – at least 10 minutes.

450g / 1lb wholemeal flour
3 tsp white sugar
Generous pinch of salt
1 level tsp baking soda
2 tsp caraway seeds
A decent pinch of saffron
4 tbsp vegan spread / butter

Method

1. Preheat the oven to 230°C / 450°F / gas mark 8 and grease or line a flat baking sheet. Make the buttermilk and leave to stand for 10 minutes.

2. In a large bowl, weigh out and then combine the flour, sugar, salt, baking soda, caraway seeds and saffron, and mix. Then add the vegan

spread and use clean hands to mix in to make a meal-like consistency. (This feels so yummy. You could do it with a fork but it honestly feels so nice to squish everything together and make the meal.)

3. When the buttermilk has curdled, make a well inside the meal and pour it in. Use a knife, not a spoon, to fold the flour in as the mix will be wet and annoying on a spoon. The dough should be quite sticky, but don't overmix it – just enough to blend it all together. Then use your hands to give it a final quick mixing, make a loaf-shaped blob and place it on the baking sheet.

4. Grease a long, sharp knife and use it to cut a deep cross in the top of loaf, edge to edge, so it appears quartered – this will help heat penetrate the bread.

5. Place in the oven on the middle shelf for 20 minutes, then turn the oven down to 200°C / 400°F / gas mark 6 and bake for another 15 minutes. When a skewer can pierce it and come out clean, it's done.

6. Leave to cool on a rack and then serve with vegan butter and cream cheese, and the first of the season's tomatoes if you can get some. Soda breads are best eaten the day they're made, the day after at the latest.

I appreciate this sounds a little chi-chi, but it really did feel special to eat this bread that I'd made just the night before, as the sun broke, while everyone else was asleep. And if you can't the bring yourself to embellish with marigold flowers, I understand.

In the home

This month we're venturing back outside to bring nature indoors. In February, our focus was on rocks and sticks, but June is a verdant and blooming month, offering new opportunities to bring nature into our homes.

Flowers are the obvious choice this month – there should be an abundance of daisies, clover and dandelions around, and none of those species will suffer if you take a flower or two. The easiest way to enjoy them is to put them in water and admire them for a day, though this is also the most wasteful.

You could take a leaf (pun intended!) from the Victorians and press them instead. Place them in tissue and pop them in between the pages of a thick book, allowing them a few weeks to dry out completely.

Once they've dried out, you could glue or sellotape them into this book, use them to make pictures or bookmarks, or if you're feeling very crafty, set them in resin to make earrings, or pendants – as ever, there are numerous tutorials available online to help you do this, and resin and jewellery fittings can easily and cheaply be bought at most craft stores.

While you're there, consider getting a block of oven-fired clay to make jewellery, coasters, or even small dishes. Collect (or ask someone to) some leaves with strong and beautiful veins and take them home. Once there, roll out the clay to the desired thickness for your project and press your leaf into it, gently rubbing until the clay takes on the pattern of the leaf. Gently peel it off and use a knife or cookie cutter to cut the clay to the shape you want. If you're making a dish, now is the time to carefully mould the sides, then place in the oven and bake according to the instructions on the clay's packaging. When it's cooled and hardened, varnish it, and put it somewhere you can enjoy it.

In your phone

We're returning to the digital clean-up work this month, and it's all about backing things up and staying secure! Go through all of your technology and make an effort to save everything to a backup source. Whether that's cloud storage, an SD card, emailing it to yourself, or some other way, make sure all of the info on your apps, all of your photos, and all of your documents are safely stored in a secondary place.

Also, change up your passwords if it's been a while. Phishing attacks and online fraud gets more sophisticated every year, and with so many of us spending so much time and storing so much information online, targets are easy to come by. Password hygiene is an effective way to limit the chances of being a victim of phishing attacks. Perhaps consider getting a password manager to manage your passwords if you don't already use one – it saves you having to remember them (and therefore having to reset them because you've forgotten them), and will prevent you from using the same password for everything. I'd recommend

Check List:

- ☐
- ☐
- ☐
- ☐
- ☐
- ☐
- ☐
- ☐

doing some research to find the one you feel most secure housing your information in.

While you're thinking about security, set up two-step security across emails, social media, and any other accounts that are vital to you, if you haven't already. And always be wary of online memes that invite you to "Discover your Star Wars/Star Trek/other popular franchise name" by combining little personal details like the surname of your first teacher, first pet's name, the road you grew up on, etc., as those are common answers to security questions and it's possible, if unlikely, that they could be harvested to hack you.

Finally, if you have the inclination, think about creating a "burner" email you can use to sign up for offers, discounts, newsletters, free trials, and anything not related to your personal or work life, so if they are ever compromised in a security breach or sold to other companies, you have less worry, and spam, to deal with!

In caring for yourself

If you've been out foraging this month, then why not use some of your spoils to infuse vodka and create your own flavoured spirits?

Elderflower vodka

An absolute favourite of mine is elderflower vodka, a delicious reminder of summer when it's finally ready, and it couldn't be simpler. Early in the morning, harvest 10–12 elderflower heads (they smell strongest the closer to dawn you gather them, so do it before the sun gets high).

Take them home, check them over for any insects, give them a quick rinse and then add them to a litre glass jar that you can seal. Add 100g / 3½ oz sugar, the zest of one lemon and a small squeeze of the juice, and 750ml / 26fl oz / 3¼ cups of vodka, and seal the jar, before giving it a good shake. Then put it in a cool, but not cold, dark place for around six weeks, until it's taken on a pale golden colour. Strain it through cheesecloth until it's clear, and then put It away again for at least two months (I know, I know!). Once it's matured, serve neat straight from the freezer or over ice, or with a delicate flavoured tonic water.

Elderflower cordial

If you don't drink alcohol, try elderflower cordial instead. For this you'll need around 25–30 elderflower heads (harvested as close to dawn as you can), 2 litres / 35fl oz / 3¼ cups boiling water, 1kg / 2lb 4oz caster (granulated) sugar, 50g / 1lb 2oz citric acid and 2 unwaxed lemons, sliced.

Rinse the elderflowers and set aside. Add the sugar to the boiling water, stir it, and let it cool. When it's cooled, add the citric acid, sliced lemons, and finally the flowers. Cover and set aside for at least 24 hours, giving it an occasional stir. Then strain it through cheesecloth into bottles. It will keep for three months in the fridge, thanks to the preserving abilities of the citric acid.

In writing

For June I have chosen **Tove Jansson's _The Summer Book_**. Jansson is best known for her nature-loving creations _The Moomins_, beloved by children in Scandinavia and beyond, but she also wrote ten adult fiction novels, of which _The Summer Book_ is one such work.

Set on an island in Finland, a six-year-old child and her grandmother are spending the summer together. The child's father is ostensibly there too, though never actually appears; he remains a figure who is mentioned but never seen. It's a gentle book, about the relationship between two people living at opposite ends of their lives, bound by blood and tradition. Together they explore the island and each other, observing migrating birds as often as they test and puzzle over why the other does or says a certain thing a certain way. It's written in Jansson's trademark disarming fashion, but it's never blunt, always delicate and kind. Kindness is a key factor in the novel – even when the two of them are at loggerheads, their battles are underscored with their desire to be kind to each other, which I think is a lesson we can all take forward. And when they unite on an adventure, what follows is a joyful exploration of the place they've found themselves, and their delight in discovering it together.

It's a dreamy book, just right for reading outside. I'd recommend packing a little picnic and taking yourself somewhere green, or near water, and whiling away a few hours reading. Or if you're staying in, recreate the experience by sitting in the sunniest patch of the room and putting a soundtrack on in the background: birdsong, a babbling brook, the sound of the sea.

Voices, past and present

June is the month of the summer solstice, when eyes around the world turn to Glastonbury to watch the sunrise behind Stonehenge. It might be one of the most popular solstice celebrations, but it's far from the only one.

In Ottawa, Canada, an annual three-day Summer Solstice Indigenous Festival takes place, jointly celebrating the longest day of the year and Canada's National Indigenous Peoples Day. The festival acknowledges it takes place on the traditional and unceded lands of the Algonquin people and their descendants, and aims to raise awareness and celebrate the contributions Inuit, First Nations and Métis people have made to Canada, as well as showcase their solstice traditions.

Midsummer in Sweden is a huge event, almost as big as Christmas, and for the weeks leading up to the solstice people begin celebrating, dancing around maypoles and gathering flowers for floral crowns. The actual solstice celebrations are family-focused, and feature much eating of herring and potatoes, and drinking of schnapps.

In Lithuania, Joninės is the name of the solstice festival, and I was lucky enough to attend a small Joninės celebration just outside of Vilnius a few years ago when I found myself there over the solstice. Drawn by the fire down by the river running outside my hotel, I went for a walk, hoping for an invite, and got one! With my new friends I sat around a fire that had to be kept burning through the night until dawn – which it was imperative we all stayed up to see – wove a very swift crown to wear out of grasses and flowers, drank beer and searched for the fern flower, which I didn't find. It was a strange, magical night and even now I can't be sure it really happened, it feels so impossible and dreamlike, which I suppose is exactly how you should feel about time spent in liminal times and places – to occupy the in-between is to be unsure of what's real and what isn't. Before Christianity was introduced, Lithuanians, who lived in close proximity to the natural world, predominantly worshipped nature deities, and that love and worship and gratitude for the natural world is still present in Joninės festivals today.

The summer solstice marks a peak, but also a transition. I think it's strange how we all see it as the beginning of summer, and bathe in all the light frivolity summer brings with it, while pushing away the knowledge that it's the point in time when the darkness starts to return, slowly at first, then rushing in like a tide as the year dies. It's an intangible time; all of the solstices are thresholds between then and now, as barriers between worlds are broken down and doorways and new paths open up.

The first thing Kiran Millwood Hargrave tells me is that she lives a five-minute walk from the river. The river in question is in Oxford, a small offshoot of the Thames sandwiched between two weirs, which protects it from dangerous currents. She hastens to tell me that it's clean – acknowledging the common Oxfordian disdain for people who attempt to swim in the main branch of the Thames, which is notoriously dirty. Kiran is an award-winning author, primarily of middle-grade fiction, but she has written for teenagers and adults too. She is also, if you hadn't already guessed, a devoted wild swimmer. Both her writing and her swimming make her someone familiar with navigating liminal spaces, moving between the thresholds of real life and the fictional, land and water, the lines between the known and unknown blurring.

Kiran's mother can't swim, so she made sure her children were confident and happy in the water, and also encouraged her to have a deep, lifelong relationship with the outdoors. Her parents are walkers – so much so their honeymoon was centred around walking Hadrian's Wall – and Kiran recalls that all of her childhood holidays had huge elements of walking to them. Her grandparents live in Norfolk, close to the sea, so the sea has been a huge part of the background of her life, too.

Though she hasn't always appreciated nature – like me, she lost her enthusiasm for it as a teenager as she worked to discover herself and whom she loved, remembering at the time how she felt nature wasn't "cool".

But that all changed when Kiran was in her early twenties.

"I got very sick with depression," she tells me, "and essentially turned to nature as part of my healing, alongside therapy and medication. It really was my saving grace, and in the past five years I've become evangelical about the benefits of nature and being outdoors."

Since then Kiran has made a concerted effort to engage with nature as much as she can. She's lucky to have a garden, and has made her office in a room that overlooks it, so even indoors she can see the families of blue tits that make their home there. More than that, she says over the past five years, as she's realized her depression is a condition she's going to have to live with, as opposed to "defeat", she's begun taking deliberate steps to get outside, going on walks multiple times per day.

"There used to be weeks where I'd never get further than the corner shop," she says. "And it's just extraordinary to me now that I had the lifestyle that would allow me to go for walks and I didn't. So now I make sure they're part of my routine."

Then she goes on to talk about the river, and her words speed up, her excitement and joy at even the thought of being in water shining through. Kiran tells me about the patch of river just five minutes from her home where she swims, and how the breathing techniques she's developed to cope with that first shock of cold water have helped her when coping with anxiety.

Another interesting thing that comes up is body image, and how in the water you feel weightless and how it's an environment she feels her body thrives in.

"It's a place where I feel protected and not judged, and when I meet other wild swimmers they're all shapes and sizes, because it's not an activity that excludes any body shape."

Kiran mostly swims with friends she's introduced to wild swimming, painting a vivid and beautiful picture of young women breaking free from the traumas and demands of modern life and joyfully chucking themselves in the river to spend a little time being wild and part of the natural world – no chlorine, no whistles, no noise. No male gaze. No expectations. It sounds deliciously bucolic, and makes me – a very weak but eager swimmer – long to put on my wetshoes and take a dip in the sea (Kiran also has a pair so maybe I'm only a few months away from becoming a wild swimmer myself).

As our conversation winds up, she returns to how much the outdoors has helped her, and how much she realizes now the importance of spending time in and appreciating nature, especially for her mental health.

"I think people who can enjoy a sunset are the happiest people alive," she muses. "Because you're never bored, and it's an incredible gift to give yourself. Even if nature might not seem your thing, step outside – both of your front door and your comfort zone – and find any green space and look at it. A lot of love comes with attention and the more you look at nature, the more you'll grow to love it."

June

In your hands

July

Regarding July

July is synonymous with holidays… if you're a human. But if you're not, then July is a real load-bearing month – literally! Hedges, trees and even garden plants are laden with flowers and fruit beginning to form.

If you've been reluctant to get out foraging before now, this is an ideal month to dally with it. Wild strawberries, chanterelle mushrooms, chickweed, yarrow, wood sorrel, nettles and dandelions are all abundant. Update your plant-identifying apps, charge your phones, pack a lunch and some water and take a bus or train to your nearest woodland and see what you can see. Alternately, for the less-confident gatherers, numerous fruit farms will have their pick-your-own services; collect a bunch of friends and spend the day picking your own farmed fruit. It still counts as being in nature – what could be more natural than hand-picking seasonal produce in the great outdoors?

Cygnets, goslings and ducklings will be abundant and they're so sweetly endearing. I maintain that it's impossible to look at ducklings and feel sad, so if you find yourself having any strife, take a shot of nature's serotonin by heading to a pond, river, lake or canal, or finding a good live feed and seeing if you can spot any ducklings. If you're in the UK and you're very lucky, you might see some hoglets (baby hedgehogs) too. First litters are born between May and July, and second through August and September. Hedgehogs are so great. Just good, sweet, snuffly, spiky little wonders.

July is a great month for lying down outside, especially in late afternoon, when the heat is beginning to die down. Even if it's rained recently, the sun and warmth should mean the ground dries off fairly quickly, so take advantage of it and throw down a blanket, cardigan or nothing at all and lie down on the ground, somewhere you feel safe. Spread your arms wide and turn your palms to the earth and feel it beneath you. Let your eyes drift closed (if they're not already) and just breathe. Listen. What can you hear? The sound of a light breeze in the grass? The calls of birds? The rustling of unknown animals? The sounds of bees droning as they go about their bee business? Isn't it lovely to lie still with the sun on your face and do nothing but lie in the grass? I hope even if getting outside is challenging for you that you're able to do this.

Once you're done lying down in the grass, have a look around for white clover blossoms, then scour the surrounding leaves for a lucky four-leafer. If you remember May's Voice with Alice Broadway, you'll know it's more than possible to find one if you look, and you don't even need a magical garden to do so! Statistically, 1 in every 10,000 clovers will have the mutation (though a survey of 5 million lowered those odds to 1 in 5,000) that gives it four leaves instead of three. And probability theory indicates that a 1.2m squared area of dense clover will contain 10,000 clovers, so theoretically you only need to search a relatively small space to find one. I set out to find one in 2020, and I did, so you can too! And who doesn't want a little extra luck?

In the skies

From 12 July to 23 August, the Delta Aquariids meteor shower is active, peaking from Aquarius on the 28–29th.

Our second supermoon of the year, a Full Buck Moon, can be seen at 18:37 GMT on 13 July.

It's known as the Buck Moon because it's the time of year bucks begin growing new antlers, preparing for the mating and rutting season later in the year. As with June's supermoon, the moon will appear bigger and brighter than usual. If you can, it's worth heading out somewhere with an unobscured view of the southeastern horizon around 10pm, to see it in its glory.

The new moon occurs at 17:55 GMT on the 28th, which means if the skies are clear and you can find somewhere with reduced light pollution, you stand an excellent chance of seeing some of the 20 meteors per hour that form the Delta Aquariids. They're formed from the debris of the comets Kracht and Marsden.

In the soil

PLANTS YOU CAN SOW THIS MONTH: Basil, chives, rosemary, lettuce, spinach – last chance for dwarf peas.

MAINTENANCE THIS MONTH: Keep an eye on the foliage on your tomatoes again, and trim it back if necessary to expose the fruits to sunlight – they won't ripen without it. Use sharp scissors or a knife to cut leaves away at the join.

Watch out for flowers on the basil – keep pinching them out before they can happen.

Keep your plants hydrated as the weather gets warmer. Don't water at night; always do it first thing in the morning so the plants aren't sitting in it overnight. And go from the bottom to deter pests and to avoid over-watering.

Keep feeding and **watering those tomatoes and chillies!** Tie up your tomatoes and chillies as they start to become heavy with fruit to keep the branches from snapping. Support them with canes if necessary.

HARVESTING THIS MONTH: Basil, chives, rosemary, spinach, baby carrots, tomatoes, strawberries, peas, spring onions (scallions), microgreens – it's a feast!

In season

July continues to be bountiful in **berries**, and **bilberries**, **blueberries**, **cherries**, **gooseberries**, **greengages** and **strawberries** are lush and ripe; **apricots** and **peaches** too. It's also melon season, which is perfect, because there is nothing more refreshing than sweet, succulent melon chunks on a ridiculously hot day. Eat them straight from the rind, or freeze them in cubes to add to your drinks, or simply to suck on when the mood takes you. But say goodbye to the kiwi fruits for a while – after seven long months serving as a hefty dose of vitamin C, this is the last month they're in season.

In our vegetable stashes we can expect a rainbow of delights, with **artichokes**, **aubergines (eggplant)**, **beetroot (beets)**, **broad (fava)**, **green** and **runner beans**, **broccoli**, **carrots**, **courgettes (zucchini)**, **fennel**, **kohlrabi**, all kinds of **lettuce**, **mangetout (snow peas)**, **new potatoes**, **peas**, **radishes**, **rocket**, **samphire**, **sea kelp**, **spinach**, **spring onions (scallions)**, **tomatoes** and **turnips**.

The idea for this recipe came after reading Rukmini Iyer's incredible *The Green Roasting Tin*. The luxury of making a beautiful dinner in one tin is a lovely thing, and this is a really nice summer evening supper for when you're a bit tired of salads but can't cope with something too heavy.

Roasted aubergine orzo

Ingredients

1 small to medium aubergine (eggplant) / summer squash /
1 decent-sized courgette (zucchini)

100g / 3½ oz dried orzo

Small onion / shallot, roughly chopped

---

2 cloves garlic, chopped lengthways in half

300ml / 10½ fl oz vegetable stock

---

1 bay leaf

---

1 tsp tarragon

Salt and pepper

---

1 tbsp olive oil

If you're not an aubergine (eggplant) fan, you could try summer squash or golden courgettes instead. You will need a deep tray for this – I have an enamel one, but any smallish roasting tin will do.

Method

1. Preheat the oven to 200°C / 400°F / gas mark 6. Wash and chop the aubergine / squash / courgette and chop into 2-inch chunks. Douse in olive oil, add salt and pepper, and roast in the oven in your roasting tin for 30 minutes.

2. Then remove and put aside on a plate. In the same tray you just roasted your veg in, add the orzo and cover in stock, before replacing the vegetables. Add the onion and garlic, the bay leaf, tarragon, salt and pepper and place in the oven. After 25 minutes, remove it, stir in the tablespoon of olive oil and put it back in the oven for 5 more minutes.

It really is that easy, and the smoky, aniseedy tarragon works so well with the sweet aubergine.

In the home

A couple of years ago there was a big and sudden boom in the creation of sourdough starters; every social media feed was swamped with pictures of starters in various states, from a day one flour-and-water gloop, all the way through to loaves of bread, fresh from the oven. And while I envied everyone their bread (in the way I instantly and furiously envy anyone who has a lot of carbs in their future), I still wasn't quite tempted enough to make my own until my friend Fox made a chocolate starter.

He'd been cultivating and baking with his regular starter for a while, and one day, while splitting it, he decided that instead of using the discard (the part you're no longer going to grow) for pancakes or pikelets, he'd use it to cultivate a second starter. This isn't too unusual; after all, lots of people give away their discard to friends and family (if you're feeling very generous you can send it off with a first feed and instructions; it makes a lovely present). But Fox cultivated his second starter with cocoa.

He made a chocolate-flavoured starter, and used it to bake a loaf of bread which, in his words, tasted like "dark, rich chocolate, stout and bitter rye".

And that was it. I began my starter that day.

If you've already got one, then congratulations, you can feel very smug and happy that you already live in a world where amazing bread is right there for the taking. If not, what follows is instructions to grow your own. Sourdough is great to bake, because once you have the starter you only need flour, salt and water to bake a loaf. And there are dozens of no-knead methods that mean making it is less labour-intensive than normal bread. The only pieces of specialist equipment you might benefit from is a cast-iron Dutch oven for the baking, three glass jars with lids (two for growing the starter and one for "discard"), and weighing scales. I didn't even have fancy baker's scales, just regular ones.

Here's how I did it.

Day 1: I added 80g / 2¾oz of plain (all-purpose) white flour and 20g / ¾oz of white rye flour to a clean jar. I then added 100ml / 3½fl oz / scant ½ cup of water and stirred it together until it was smooth. I placed the lid on top of the jar but didn't fasten it – you want some air to get in, but not too much. Let it rest for a full 24 hours (for this reason it's a good idea to begin in the morning; I chose 10am).

Day 2: After 24 hours give it another stir, then cover and rest for 24 hours.

Day 3: This is when the work begins (for you; the yeast is way ahead of you). Measure out 80g / 2¾oz plain flour and 20g / ¾oz of rye flour into a bowl, and 100ml / 3½fl oz / scant ½ cup of water. Then place a second, clean jar, onto the scale, and zero it. Once the scale is zeroed, carefully pour in 50g/1¾oz of your starter. To this 50g, add the flour mixture and the water, and stir it smooth. Place the lid on top – again, not fastening it – and put it aside for 24 hours.

This process is the same for Days 4–7. Separate, add fresh flour and water, and stir. As for the other 50g, you can add that to the third clean jar, and let it become your discard jar.

For some people, you may be ready to bake after Day 7, in which case you can stop the daily feeding. Personally, my starter was still a little weak until Day 14 (!), so I kept going with the flour and water, repeating the process every day, until it was eventually strong enough. How did I know? Two ways. Firstly, sometime after Day 4, you'll start to notice the volume of your starter rises and falls. (If this doesn't happen until Day 6, 7 or even 8, don't panic! It's all about the natural yeast in the air around you getting into the flour and water mix. Sometimes it takes a while for enough to accumulate.) I used a marker to mark my jar with the volume just after feeding, and then again at hourly intervals, so I could see where it peaked and how long it took to get there, and how long it took to fall.

Once it repeated the pattern three days in a row, I felt sure it was viable. The second way is to drop a teaspoonful in water – if it floats, it's ready!

When your starter is established, unless you are baking with it two or three times a week, you can store it in the fridge, which slows down its feeding rate so you can just feed it once a week. If you keep it in the fridge, get it out before you plan to use it and let it come to room temperature before feeding it pre-use, then feed it again after you've taken some to bake with, and leave it out for a few hours before you put it back in.

You should also keep your discard jar in the fridge, and you don't need to feed this one, not even before you use it! Instead, feel free to keep adding to it, and use it to bake with. There are loads of recipes online for sourdough crackers, crumpets, muffins, cookies, banana bread and all kinds of things that are quick and easy. For the first two weeks of growing my starter I had fresh bakes every day in a bid to use up my discard, and I still make crackers at least twice a week.

For crackers: 250g of starter discard, 2 tbsp of good extra virgin olive oil, salt, chilli flakes, whisk until mixed then spread a 5mm layer on greaseproof paper. Bake at 160°C/320°F/gas mark 3 for 10 minutes, remove from the oven and score into cracker-size segments, then put them back in the oven for 25 minutes. Listen to them snap apart naturally as they cool!

There are also dozens of sourdough bread recipes available online too – I favour a no-knead one that takes a while but always makes good bread. And be sure to troubleshoot online too if you're worried about your starter. It can be daunting at first, but it's so worth it. No other sourdough in the world will taste quite like yours!

In your phone

During the big mindfulness boom late last decade, guided meditation was one of the self-care trends to make a real comeback. Once almost exclusively the province of New Age thinkers, the act of following a guided meditation and visualizing yourself into a state of calm became part of a daily morning routine for many, as common as cornflakes or checking the weather. Like a lot of people who felt wrung out by modern life, I tried it. Meditation isn't right for everyone – it can trigger anxiety attacks in some people, and the actual act of meditating didn't stick for me as I couldn't focus, but one thing that did stick was becoming aware of my breathing, and learning to breathe with intent.

Like a lot of people who have never suffered from breathing problems, how I got my oxygen wasn't something I paid much attention to, happy to let my lungs and brain do all of the heavy lifting, until I noticed after I finished a meditation session that I felt energized, as well as calm and focused. After doing a little digging and a little self-experimenting, I realized it wasn't visualizing forests and oceans that led to this state of active awareness, but the act of controlled and deliberate breathing. So that was the bit I kept in my daily routine.

And because it's the 21st century, there is an app for it. Lots, in fact! Breathly, Prana Breath and Breath Ball are all highly rated, and I recommend, as with the other apps, that you try a few out and see which one you like best. Then set aside five minutes a day when you can breathe mindfully. The beginning and end of the day are the most obvious times, but maybe try it at lunchtime, or mid-afternoon if you find your energy slumping and you need a boost.

In caring for yourself

Lavender flowers through June and July, so they're ideal months to make lavender sachets to put in your drawers to deter common clothes moths, or to make your knickers smell nice, or to give to people as presents, or to carry around to inhale every now and then. Moths sound like a problem from the past, recalling camphor mothballs and very old houses, but common clothes moths are still a potential annoyance even these days. They like to lay their eggs in natural materials like wool, and when the larvae hatch, they begin eating them, leading to holes. A rise in synthetic clothing has reduced their "hunting ground", but on the off-chance you do have woollen knitwear then it's a good idea to protect it, and lavender smells strong enough to deter the moths from using your jumpers as daycare.

There are numerous ways to make the sachets – I like to use cheesecloth that I sew into little packets, but you can use old clothes you've cut up, remnants of fabric you have lying around, or even those little taffeta bags that wedding favours come in, and you can make them as pretty or fancy as you like, adding ribbons and embellishments.

If you're using taffeta bags, it really couldn't be easier: just pour in around two heaped teaspoons of dried lavender flowers, pull the ribbons and tie in a double knot and you're done. Fling them in your drawers, hang them from the hangers in your wardrobe, and go and make some tea.

If you've decided to sew, it will take a little longer. What I do is cut out a rectangle of cheesecloth, around 6 x 3.5 inches, and fold it in half. I sew two of the three open sides up, leaving a lip of around 5mm. I then turn the little pocket inside out, stuff it with two or three heaped teaspoons of dried lavender and sew the top shut. I then sew a small piece of ribbon to the top to cover my inevitably messy stitching and to make them look pretty, and they're done.

You can buy dried lavender with relative ease online, though try to buy from a reputable site or direct from a lavender farm, as not all dried lavender is equal and older buds will have a fainter smell. Or you can dry your own if you've grown some by cutting it off the plant and hanging it upside down in small bunches for 2–3 weeks somewhere warm, until thoroughly dried.

To keep them smelling great throughout the year, I add a few drops of lavender essential oil every once in a while, once the natural scent has started to fade.

In writing

Shortlisted for the Wainwright Prize, **Jini Reddy's Wanderland** is a homage to the landscape of the UK. It's probably the most esoteric entry in the book club as it very much focuses on the magic of the land and engaging with nature as a force, or energy. Reddy was born to Indian parents living in South Africa, who fled to the UK during apartheid, but despite being born in London she still feels a sense of being an "outsider". To combat that, she forges her own connections with the land in Britain.

In her first book, *Wild Times*, she did this physically – trying out bush craft, foraging, horse-whispering and stargazing, among other things – seeking tangible connections with nature and the outdoors using the five common senses. *Wanderland* sees Reddy connecting to nature with her internal voice, and starting a conversation with it; listening and following, opening herself up to "hear" what it has to say.

It's a brilliant, beautiful book about letting go of the physical, and your preconceptions of the world and how it works, and opening your heart and mind to the possibility there's more to the land around us than we can touch, hear, smell, taste and see. Even if you're not open to the idea of hidden frequencies and the idea of nature having a real spirit, it's a glorious and joyful exploration of the countryside and embracing the idea that perhaps all things are possible, if we allow them to be. That in order to really be part of the natural world, we have to open up and let it in.

Voices, past and present

There is a Manx tale called **Tehi Tegi** about an enchantress who can turn herself into a bat. She is beautiful, supernaturally so, and of course every man she comes across falls head over heels in love with her, much to the annoyance of the island's womenfolk.

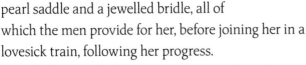

Once every man on the island is besotted, and utterly devoted to fulfilling her every desire, she decides to ride through the land on a milk-white horse, demanding gold horseshoes, a mother-of-pearl saddle and a jewelled bridle, all of which the men provide for her, before joining her in a lovesick train, following her progress.

Tehi Tegi leads the men to a river, and uses her magic to make them believe they can easily cross it. But of course, they can't, and they all drown. Meanwhile, Tehi Tegi transforms herself into a bat (or, in some versions, a wren) and takes to the skies, leaving the women of Man bereft (or liberated?).

Bats are inextricably connected to dark and dangerous things, from folk tales about them getting caught in girls' hair and carrying off strands, to Dracula and the vampire myths, to very real vampire bats, and of course the rising discourse about bats as disease vectors when humans encroach on their habitats. But bats are actually brilliant and vital members of every ecosystem they inhabit, making sure insect populations stay balanced. Bat species account for around one-fifth of all mammal species (there are over 1,100 types known so far), and they have very sweet faces. All right, that's more of an opinion than a fact, but I stand by it.

Tilly Latimer has my dream job. Or at least one of them. She grew up in rural north Dorset, and now lives near Bristol, in the southwest, where she works as a professional ecological consultant, a role she's held for the past 17 years. She is a lifelong student of nature; her Bachelor's degree is in Biology and her Masters in Restoration Ecology of Terrestrial and Aquatic Environments ("What a mouthful!" she adds gleefully).

Tilly has worked across the entire ecology industry, and even her hobbies take her outside: she met her husband at their university mountaineering club, she rides her own horse, and their family holidays revolve around being outdoors as much as possible. Nature is, quite simply, her life.

"My relationship with nature is probably very different from most people's because it also pays my mortgage," she acknowledges. "And I'm aware of the politics of nature too, because a lot of my work hinges on the policies and laws put into place by the government. I'm reliant on nature to make a living and if that was ever taken away then the likelihood is that I'd end up doing a desk job somewhere, probably in a completely different industry."

On the rare occasions she's not outdoors, either for work or fun, she's reading about it, keeping up to date on issues and policy in the natural world.

"I'm very privileged that this is my life," she says, "though there are downsides to it."

The work is seasonal; from March through October it doesn't stop and she earns the majority of her income then, which means strict budgets have to be employed throughout the rest of the year.

Then there's the lack of sleep. During the summer months Tilly often spends her nights counting bats, which are notoriously nocturnal. It means she often operates on around three hours' sleep while she's surveying bat populations. There are other sacrifices too: birthdays, weddings, numerous occasions that she can't attend because nature doesn't take days off – and the weather also has to be factored in: bad weather means surveys need to be rearranged, and so her personal life is effectively on hold during the surveying season.

It might be enough to put someone else off, but not Tilly.

"Nature is so interwoven into my life that I think the fabric of my life would fall apart without it."

Despite that, becoming an ecologist wasn't always the plan. Initially, she'd toyed with the idea of being a vet: "Like a lot of ecologists, I'm a failed vet!" she jokes. But then she goes on to explain that she chose a degree in biology because she knew a science degree would open doors to pretty much any job she wanted, whereas an arts or humanities one would make a role in a scientific field harder to secure. It's definitely paid off, she feels; as well as giving her a living, she finds being outside is the best way to clear her head and maintain her physical and mental wellness.

She acknowledges that nature, especially the kind of nature that she deals with, can be overwhelming to people who haven't had the experiences she's had.

"A lot of the time, when people live in cities, the green spaces they encounter can be manicured and managed, so it can be quite intimidating to get out into the slightly wilder spaces, but those are the ones where I think you get the real interesting things. So I would say to go anywhere it's green and expand your experiences from there. If you can go to a local park, you can probably do a little moorland walk, if you can get to some."

July

In your hands

August

Regarding August

We always think of September as being the month the trees and plants begin to turn gold, but if you look carefully, you'll see it starts before then. As the days begin to get shorter, August is the month when you can really start to see the changes. Which, if you're anything like me, you'll find deeply reassuring.

I used to hate the last two weeks of August more than any other time of year – even January, even February – because those final two weeks of summer felt like stasis. By then I'd explored everywhere worth exploring and I'd exhausted all my usual distractions. The much longed-for summer holidays were outstaying their welcome, and it wasn't that I wanted to go back to school so much as I wanted *change*. I was ready for it, could feel it like I was trapped inside a smaller version of myself, desperate to shed my skin. I think a lot of nature feels the same way in August, too. Look at the birds who start to line up along the telephone wires, anxious to fly south even though summer is still in full swing here. Look at the baby animals straying farther and farther from their parents, aching for independence. Look at the leaves, slowly starting to edge out away from green into gold.

The fact is, no one is really sure *why* leaves change colour over autumn and winter, only *how,* and it's the *how* that leads us to assume the *why* is to do with fading light. Weaker sunlight in autumn and winter offers the trees fewer opportunities to produce chlorophyll (the pigment that makes them appear green), so they produce less, and in turn the carotenoids (the same pigments that make corn yellow and carrots orange) are revealed. So, in very simple terms, the summer greenery is like makeup – a coat of emerald over a golden surface. In autumn we can see the other colours that chlorophyll masks: the ochres and golds of carotenoids, and the reds of flavonoids, which are only produced in response to lowering temperatures. There are some scientists who think that leaf colour change used to be more important, maybe even to attract insects that are now extinct, but that tree evolution is so slow it hasn't caught up yet.

Another kind of stasis. But the trees, like me, like us, will get there in the end.

There are still plenty of distractions to be had. Flowers will give way to berries; blackberries, rosehips and elderberries are all in season. If you're going foraging please make sure to use a guide (or two, or three) to be sure what you're picking is what you think it is, and pick berries from above waist height to avoid any that have been marked by either wild or domestic animals. In the UK, cobnuts will be on bushes too; I used to harvest them by the dozen as a child and run rampant with pockets full of them. They're a kind of hazelnut and they look like it too: soft brown oval nuts in green husks with frilly tops. You can eat the young ones raw;

the older ones are better toasted. In both the UK and the US crabapples will be around too, and while they're very sour, they do make good crabapple jelly, or can be used in crabapple gin or vodka, for the spiritually minded among you. Rowan berries (mountain ash) are also incredibly bitter if eaten raw, but can be used to make jellies and jams too (or try your hand at rowan schnapps!). If the weather is cool and wet, mushroom rings will start to appear in fields, meadows, gardens and public parks – dance in them if you dare.

Wildlife-wise, young foxes are getting more and more independent, and city foxes are already very curious, so keep an eye out for them shadowing your walk home. In fact a lot of young animals will be taking their first real steps into adult life, so see if you can find a spot in a wood, or by a river, and quietly observe. Months behind the majority of the natural world, it's grasshopper mating season, so listen out for them. Keep an eye on the daytime skies too as migrations begin; the last of the cuckoos will be leaving the UK, and swifts will also start to go, along with the early swallows, nightingales and turtle doves. In the US, hummingbirds will start to move south, save for Anna's hummingbird, which stays year-round in its home in the west.

Make the most of the last days of summer by spending as much time as you can outside. Meet up with friends and family for picnics, either doorstep or more traditional. Go for long walks between pubs or cafés wearing holes in your shoes. Take your lunch to a local park. Enjoy it, because soon it will be gone.

In the skies

The final **supermoon of the year happens at 01:35 GMT on 12 August,** so if you missed the other two, or were thwarted by clouds, then this is your last chance to see a supermoon in 2022. The August moon is known as the Sturgeon Moon, as the Native Americans who named it felt that this time of year was the easiest time to catch sturgeon in the Great Lakes. Other tribes knew it as the Green Corn Moon – the last moon before the corn was ready to harvest.

The **12th and 13th of August** also sees the peak of the **Perseids** – usually one of the best and most reliable meteor showers in the calendar. Unfortunately, the full moon means even with clear skies only the brightest meteors will be visible, a severe reduction on the 60 per hour we can expect during the peak. But the Perseids actually occur from 17 July to 24 August, a crossover with the Delta Aquariids, so eyes to the skies during this period and you'll surely see something. The Perseids will radiate from Perseus, and the Delta Aquariids from Aquarius if you want to be a little more certain about which shower you're seeing meteors from.

August's **new moon occurs at 08:17 GMT on the 27th,** which is also a **great night to spot Mercury.** It's at its greatest eastern elongation, so look low in the western skies just after sunset. If the skies are cloudy, don't worry: it'll have its greatest western elongation in October, which is the best time to spot this tiny planet.

Saturn will also be visible this month, at opposition; on the 14th it'll be fully illuminated by the sun and at its closest to the Earth. With a telescope you'll be able to see it and some of its moons, but the naked eye will be able to find it easily too.

Check List:

- ☐
- ☐
- ☐
- ☐
- ☐
- ☐
- ☐
- ☐

In the soil

PLANTS YOU CAN SOW THIS MONTH:
Basil, chives, rosemary (all indoors),
spinach, salad leaves (keep the latter
two in the shade!)

MAINTENANCE THIS MONTH:
Continue monitoring the foliage on
your tomatoes, trimming it back if
necessary to expose the fruits to
sunlight – they won't ripen without it.
Use sharp scissors or a knife to cut
leaves away at the join. Watch out for
flowers on the basil – keep pinching
them out before they can happen. If
your peas are outside, watch out for
pea moth caterpillars. The moth lays
its eggs inside the pods through June
and July.

HARVESTING THIS MONTH: Basil,
chives, rosemary, spinach, baby
carrots, tomatoes, strawberries, spring
onions (scallions), peas, microgreens.

In season

We are spoiled in August, with a ridiculous and diverse amount of fresh fruit and vegetables available to us.

Bilberries, blueberries, cherries, damsons, greengages, strawberries, peaches, the first **nectarines, plums, raspberries** and **redcurrants. Figs** and **loganberries** are in season too.

Vegetables patches yield **artichokes, aubergines (eggplant), beetroot (beets), broad (fava), green and runner beans, broccoli, carrots, courgettes (zucchini), fennel, kohlrabi,** all kinds of **lettuce, mangetout (snow peas), potatoes, pak choi, peas, radishes, rocket, samphire, spinach, spring onions (scallions), tomatoes** and **turnips. Sweetcorn, peppers** and **marrows** are newly in season too, and so are early **mushrooms.**

I find August makes me both restless and lethargic. I didn't like it as a child, the novelty of the endless days of no school wearing off; I was listless and languid, wilting in fields that were too hot to explore and wishing I could burrow into the cool earth and wait for nightfall. As adults we don't get the long summer holiday, but I think the relentless sunshine and heat can start to tire us out, especially in tandem with our busy lives. So August's dish is a lively but light salad, from Tuscany – a place that knows a thing or two about coping with heat – that can be easily thrown together without making you want to lie down on the kitchen floor and wish for September. And if you started growing your own tomatoes and basil, this is the dish to use them in.

Tuscan bread and tomato salad

Ingredients

Good olive oil

Hald a ciabatta / sourdough boule, the staler the better, torn into bite-size chunks

---

2 garlic cloves, lightly crushed so they holds their shape

---

1 x 400g / 14oz can butter beans, drained

150g / 5½ oz mix of tomatoes, roughly chopped; I like to use home-grown sweet cherry toms along with bigger heirloom ones. If you can get a mix of sizes and colours, go for it, but if not then pick your favourite kind and work with those.

---

1 yellow pepper, roughly chopped

---

1 red onion, finely chopped

Artichoke hearts (jarred) – optional, but delicious

---

2 tbsp capers

Freshly squeezed lemon juice

Salt and pepper

Fresh basil leaves

Method

1. Heat a tablespoon of oil in a wok or skillet and then turn the heat down to medium and add the bread and garlic, lightly frying it until it's golden and slightly crispy. Remove the bread from the pan and place it on kitchen roll or a towel to soak off the excess oil. Toss the beans in and lightly sauté them for a few minutes until just starting to crisp and brown. Take off the heat.

2. In a bowl, mix the tomatoes, yellow pepper, red onion, artichokes, capers, butter beans and warm garlic together, along with another glug of olive oil, your freshly squeezed lemon juice, salt and pepper. When thoroughly mixed, tear the basil and throw them in before finally adding the still-warm bread.

Then all you have to do is eat it.

In the home

This month we're going to look at how we can make our homes more sustainable, and I'm going to share with you some of the best tips to make your home and everyday life a little greener, and a little more planet-friendly. And the best thing is, a lot of energy-saving and greening tips end up saving you money too, so everyone wins.

- One of the most common tips is to consider changing your energy supplier to a greener one. There are numerous comparison websites available, so if you find yourself indoors because the sun is too hot, why not make a nice cool glass of something and do a little research (make sure to talk to your housemates/landlord if necessary before you make any changes).

- If you haven't already, swap out your lightbulbs for energy-saving ones, and of course don't leave lights on if they're not being used.

- Unplug devices that aren't being used, and stop leaving electrical goods on standby.

- Change up the way you wash your clothes: don't put a wash on unless you have a full load, use eco settings on machines if you have them, and, especially while the weather is nice, allow clothes to air dry instead of using drying machines.

- If you drink dairy milk, consider getting it delivered if possible – the glass bottles are reused, making it preferable to plastic bottles, and a lot of milk deliverers now also deliver eggs, potatoes and various other foodstuffs!

- Subscribe to a veg box; they focus on seasonal veg and it'll cut down on your plastic waste.

- You can also save some vegetable scraps to make your own stock. I keep a ziplock bag in the freezer and add carrot peels, celery and onions, but you can also use small amounts of most peels (starchy veg will make a starchy stock and cruciferous veg can make it bitter).

- If possible, buy pasta, rice, pulses, cereals, flours, etc. from stores that have refill options to reduce plastic and packaging waste.

- Consider going plant-based, at least one or two days a week. Changing diet is the biggest way an individual can help combat the climate disaster; intensive beef and dairy farming is one of the industries wreaking the most havoc on the planet. If you simply can't bear to go a day without meat of some kind, try to buy organic and as locally as possible.

- Swap out detergents and washing liquids for eco-friendly versions.

- Stop buying disposable sponges and wipes. Consider buying cloths that can be washed in the laundry and reused over and over, or knitting your own scrubbers from jute string – it's very cheap, biodegradable, and with a little bicarbonate of soda paste makes for a vigorous cleaning device!

- Also consider ditching disposable razors and buying a safety razor and replaceable blades. Why not look at bamboo toothbrushes and cotton swabs while you do.

- Recycle diligently and do a little research into local schemes for things that seem impossible to recycle, like batteries, plastic bags, razor blades, toothpaste tubes, medication blister packs, etc.

- If you have a cistern toilet, think about getting a water-saving device to go in it to reduce the amount of water you use each flush. Or make your own: I have a litre bottle full of water that's been sitting in my cistern for three years now, saving me and the planet a litre of water every time I flush.

- You can also buy water-saving shower heads or widgets to use. And while we're at it, maybe the height of summer isn't the right time to raise this, but have you considered showering less? On average, five litres of water is used every minute of a shower, so if you can cut the amount of showers you have, or the amount of time you spend in there, you can save yourself some money, and save the planet a little, too.

These are all just points to consider. But as I said at the beginning of this section, an exciting thing about making these adjustments is the benefits to you, as well as the earth.

In your phone

Well, it was bound to happen sometime. And here it is: the dreaded holiday from technology. Don't worry, I'm not going to ask you to lock your phone away for a month, or even for a day. We live in the 21st century, and like it or not, the little computers we carry around with us pretty much run our lives. But, for all their efficiency and access to information, they can be very distracting, so I'm going to gently suggest a few ways we can take brief breaks from our phones.

One thing I do is put my phone into flight mode when I'm in bed. I don't turn it off, because it's also my alarm, but I do make a conscious choice to stop receiving notifications for a while. Obviously, this might not work for you: if there are people who need to be able to reach you at any time, this is not a good idea. But if you can do it, try putting it on flight mode and leaving it that way until you've had a shower, had tea/coffee, journalled, exercised, or whatever else you do first thing in the morning. Flight mode means you don't see any notifications, so it doesn't feel as if anything urgently needs your attention. If you can manage an extra half an hour to an hour each morning without it, you might find, like me, that your mornings seem a little calmer, and that you feel more in control of them.

If you're feeling brave (and it's safe and practical to do so), why not try leaving your phone at home when you go on a walk. It means you won't be able to take any photos of anything you see, but it also means you might see something you wouldn't have done if you'd been distracted by it! Sometimes it's nice to feel disconnected – especially if it's your choice. To be outside, and focused only on that.

If that feels too far, then how about just leaving it in another room, if you can. Or if you live in a shared house and it isn't practical to leave it somewhere else, why not shut it in a drawer or put it in a bag for an hour. Out of sight, out of mind. It's not forever, just a holiday.

In caring for yourself

This month we're going to make a cooling foot cream to refresh and soothe our feet after they've been crammed inside our shoes all day. The recipe is virtually identical to the body butter we made earlier in the year, except we use soothing peppermint oil to help keep our feet feeling fresh!

Cooling foot cream
100g / 3½ oz shea butter

2 tbsp sweet almond oil

2 tbsp coconut oil

10-15 drops of peppermint oil

Clean and sterilized glass jar

Place a heatproof bowl in a large saucepan full of hot water on the hob, and keep the water warm, but not boiling. Break up the shea butter and add it to the bowl, stirring with a clean wooden spoon until it's melted. Add the sweet almond oil and the coconut oil, and mix together.

To this mixture add your peppermint oil and stir it in, put it in the fridge to cool, then, as before, beat the mixture until it's light and airy, before pouring into your glass jar. Keep it in the fridge for extra cooling powers, and use within a week.

In writing

I've chosen one of my favourite fiction books for August, in the hope you'll find the power in it that I did. The book is **Madeline Miller's *Circe***, the story of the goddess and witch who warranted nothing more than a brief mention in Homer's *Odyssey*.

What Miller does is take this barely spoken-of goddess and give her a story of her own. Using the little that's written about Circe, she weaves an epic tale of the daughter of a water god who fits her skin better on land, who is easier in the company of animals than in people, and who works and toils to learn the secrets of herbs and flowers to become the most powerful witch of her time. Yes, there's romance and Greek drama (the gods are involved, of course there's Greek drama), but more than anything it's a book about finding your way to who you're supposed to be, through nature. And that's why we're here, after all. So if you haven't already read it, I invite you to. And if you have, I invite you to use these languid August days to do it again. Let's embrace our inner witches and retreat to our own islands of nature and magic.

Voices, past and present

One of my favourite English folk stories is the green children of Woolpit, which was said to take place around harvest time in the 12th century. One late summer morning the villagers of Woolpit, in Suffolk, were astonished to find two green-skinned children, one male and one female, dressed in strange clothing, beside one of the wolf trapping pits the village was named for. They were taken to the home of Sir Richard de Calne, where they spoke in their own strange language and refused to eat any of the food put before them, until they came across broad beans (fava beans), which they ate eagerly. As time passed, they were persuaded to eat other food, until they adapted to a "normal" human diet, and the green tint to their skin was lost. Sadly, both children sickened after being baptized as Christians and the boy child died, though his sister eventually rallied and survived.

His sister learned to speak English, and so was able to explain to her foster father that she came from St Martin's Land, and she and her brother had found their way into our world when they'd been herding their cattle. She said they'd heard a loud noise (thought to have been the bell at the church of Bury St Edmunds), and suddenly found themselves beside the wolf pit where they were found.

She told incredible stories about St Martin's Land: that the sun there never shone, that it was always twilight, and everyone there was green-skinned, as she had been. She said there was another, luminous land across the river from St Martin's Land, but it did not sound as though she'd been there. She eventually took the name Agnes and lived as a servant for de Calne, though she was known for being "impudent and wanton". She eventually married the archdeacon of Ely, Richard Barre, who worked for Henry II, and I guess after that she lived out a normal human life, because there are no more tales about her, or any other green children.

There are lots of theories to explain the children – some supernatural and others mundane – but I won't go into them here. You can look them up yourself, or not. I prefer the mystery, the idea that somewhere is a place of perpetual twilight, where green-skinned people live in a world adjacent to ours, somewhere just out of time.

August's Voice, **writer and podcast host Laura Elliott,** says she grew up "in a house that was literally in the woods, so most of my childhood was making dens in trees, digging though dirt and collecting bones, and we used to sneak into farmer's fields and eat peas from the stalks. All of those idyllic little endeavors."

It's these words that make me remember the story of the green children for the first time in years; the wildness of them, their eager closeness to nature, and their sadness as they lost their place in it, exchanging it for the adult, normal world. Like Peter Pan, it's not so much a Fortean tale of another world, but a parable for the way we all have to grow up and lose our wildness if we want to be part of society. Laura was lucky, because living so close to the wildness of the moors in the north of England meant she didn't have to give up her wildness as early or as quickly as many others do. But Laura became ill in 2015, ending up housebound for the vast majority of her time, and realized she was losing touch with that part of herself, her rhythm with nature.

The realization was profound.

"The way we mark time is really unnatural, with clocks, and meetings, and start times and end times, but without those things, when you are just stuck at home, you start to feel cast adrift and you find years just fly by and you can't really get a handle on where time's going. And even if you can look outside and see the seasons changing, it's still really disconnecting when you're not in them."

Laura's answer to this was to bring nature to her, so she could take part in the changing of the seasons and mark the passage of time in a tactile, hands-on way. She started growing, throwing herself into the innate routines of plants, learning that each one needed sowing, tending, cutting, repotting at different times, that all of the plants she grew had different patterns of care and needs and she had to mark them to make them grow.

Now she has windowsill gardens, which as well as keeping her connected to the natural world, also allow her to feel as though she's contributing to the running of the house, which, due to her condition, largely falls to her partner.

"Growing things is my way of being involved in keeping us fed." And it's contagious. "Now we're working on making the garden a haven for wildlife, so I can sit out in it, and keeping a small veg plot. I design the layout while James [Laura's partner] does the heavy lifting. I mark out areas of grass to grow wild, choose plants to attract pollinators and decide where to put them, and think about how the garden works year-round, cultivating ivy for autumn pollinators, plants that fruit in winter for birds."

Laura got the idea from one of the few short outdoor walks she can make these days. On route to her doctor she spotted a tiny garden that has won awards for being a remarkable natural habitat, always active with insects and birds, and decided she wanted to create something similar, that she could deliberately and mindfully cultivate and enjoy.

"Before I got ill, I was obsessed with living life with a capital L. I never stopped to draw breath. I worked 90-hour weeks and the pace just wasn't sustainable. It's one of the things about life today: everyone feels like they have to achieve by X age, everything is on social media, and it's fast and it's frenetic and I don't think it's sustainable for a lot of people. The pace we set isn't a natural way of living. So for me, reconnecting with nature was what I needed to feel part of something that wasn't just pushing myself to the point of burnout."

Laura feels very strongly that one of the things we're all missing from our busy lives today is the fact we don't put roots down anymore, by which she means our lifestyles have made us strangers to nature.

"Growing things is literally putting roots down, and you don't need to buy a house or be settled to feel connected to the place you're in if you're growing things. And anyone can grow a little herb garden on a windowsill."

August

In your hands

September

Regarding September

September feels like change and there's just no escaping it. For me it starts in the last few days of August, this spark or awareness in the air, a kind of electricity, a sense of gentle hurrying: "Come on, get ready, September is almost here!"

I don't know if it's leftover from school days, when obviously September meant a return to structure and routine after the wild days of summer, or whether it's something older and more primitive than that; the realization that it's time to bring in the crops, start preserving the harvest, mend the fences and begin chopping the wood for winter. The awareness that the days are getting shorter and the still, warm air has given way to winds that nip and bite with curious teeth. Summer isn't quite over yet, but it's definitely started its circuit of goodbyes, shaking everyone's hand as it tries to head toward the door. Normally it can be persuaded to stay for one last drink, but no more than that.

The sense of getting back to business is reflected in the natural world too. Young animals that are old enough to strike out alone are encouraged to do so (gently at first, but there will be tears later); most of the migrating birds have already gone; hibernating animals are starting to prepare their burrows and dens; squirrels are storing up food to last them through the winter. Even in beehives things are changing: the worker bees are chucking the male drones out and the Queen has stopped laying eggs, with all resources going toward surviving the colder months.

The hedgerows are starting to look quite rich; there should be blackberries around for the taking; rosehips, sloes and elderberries, too. Leave the hawthorn berries (haws) where they are for now – they're better when they're riper, if you fancy making haw ketchup. In the UK, nuts abound: hazelnuts, sweet chestnuts, horse chestnuts (not edible, but can be used in soap-making and as laundry detergent as they contain saponins, though please bear in mind modern machines are developed with modern detergents in mind and all-natural ones might present their mechanics with challenges), acorns (which CAN be eaten, though will need water leaching to do so), walnuts and beech nuts, too (you'll have to fight the squirrels for those). As ever, only take a little; leave more than enough for the animals and insects that can't pop to Tesco when the cupboards run low.

In the US, wild walnuts and hazelnuts are a possibility, but please check local laws before foraging anything as they can vary at both state and municipal level.

It's also a good time to forage mushrooms, but please don't do this without the guidance of an expert – there are over 50 types of poisonous mushroom in the UK, and at least 250 in the US, and many are easily mistaken for harmless ones. By all means dance in a fairy ring, but don't pick them unless you know what you're doing. If it's something you're interested in, I'd suggest contacting local groups and going out with them, as they'll know the area and the variety of fungi available in the locale.

I always feel like whatever August took out of me, September puts right back in. Perhaps it's the legacy of school days and that feeling of a fresh start, a shiny new pencil case full of untested, unused pens. The lovely potential of it, like a clear sky after a storm.

Make the most of the golden days of September, because the autumn equinox is coming and after that the darkness rules. Though that's not necessarily a bad thing…

In the skies

The **Corn Moon occurs at 09:59 GMT on the 10th**, and is also known as the **Harvest Moon,** because it is the moon that occurs closest to the harvest.

Another good month for planet spotting, the 16th sees Neptune at opposition to the sun, as a tiny blue dot. To see it any clearer you'll need a telescope, I'm afraid. Jupiter, however, is at opposition to the sun on the 26th and will be easily spotted as it'll be the brightest spot in the sky.

Finding it will be made easier by the **new moon occurring at 21:45 GMT on the 25th,** rendering the skies dark.

The **autumn equinox takes place at 01:04 GMT on the 23rd.** The official beginning of autumn in the northern hemisphere, there will be near enough equal amounts of day and night before the dark season begins.

In the soil

PLANTS YOU CAN SOW THIS MONTH: Herbs indoors, if you have the light and heat available for them.

MAINTENANCE THIS MONTH: Watch out for flowers on the basil – keep pinching them out before they can happen.

It's time to say goodbye to your old plants if they're annuals. I break down my tomato and pea plants and use them for compost to feed my soil over winter, so it's ready to go in spring. I also save what soil I can, shaking it free from roots and feeding it compost tea. With my outdoor pots I cover them over with plastic bags to keep unwanted plants from growing and using up the nutrients in the soil, occasionally adding some compost tea. Soil is a resource – the gardeners' most valuable resource – and so it's important to take care of it, and to cherish it. Clean out any old pots you're not using and put them away for next year, wash your tools, your stakes and anything else you've used. If you've got seeds hanging around do yourself a favour and put them in labelled envelopes for next year.

HARVESTING THIS MONTH: Basil, chives, mint, rosemary, spinach, carrots, the last of the tomatoes and spring onions (scallions), microgreens.

In season

An embarrassment of natural riches is available in September – it's truly the most bountiful month.

In the fruit bowl we have **bilberries, damsons, plums, raspberries, redcurrants, figs, nectarines, melons** and **peaches**. And newly in season, **apples** are back! Along with **blackberries** (the classic apple and blackberry pairing is one to exploit), **elderberries, medlars, pears, sloes** and **grapes**.

Vegetable offerings include **artichoke, aubergines (eggplant), beetroot (beets), green and runner beans, broccoli, carrots, courgettes (zucchini), cucumber, fennel, kale, kohlrabi,** all kinds of **lettuce, mangetout (snow peas), marrow, pak choi, potatoes, peppers, radishes, rocket, sweetcorn, spring onions (scallions), tomatoes** and **turnips. Kale, leeks** and **celeriac** are back! **Mushrooms** and **celery** are in season! **Pumpkins** and **squashes** too! September spoils us.

September's recipe is for fruit hand pies, and is a great way of using up the last of the soft berries. This recipe uses apples, peaches and raspberries, but you can use blackberries, strawberries, blueberries, gooseberries or whatever else you have or can get. You can even make your own pastry if you want to (I never do). This recipe will make around six hand pies. I like to eat them outside at sunset.

Mabon hand pies

Ingredients

3 hard green apples (Granny Smiths are ideal, you don't need cooking apples), peeled, cored and chopped into roughly 1cm chunks

---

30ml / 1fl oz / 2 tbsp water

100g / 3½oz brown sugar

---

1 tsp dried cinnamon, nutmeg and cardamom combined

½ tsp dried/fresh rosemary

Freshly squeezed lemon juice

---

2 peaches, stones removed and chopped into rough chunks

120g / 4¼oz raspberries

---

2 sheets pre-rolled puff pastry (remove from the fridge half an hour before you begin!)

Method

1. Add the chopped apples to a stainless-steel pan, along with the water, brown sugar, spice mix, rosemary and lemon juice, and slowly, gently heat. Stir occasionally.

2. When the apples are soft and caramelized, remove from the heat and

leave to cool slightly, but not completely. You might find it helps to spread them out in a clean roasting tin.

3. While the apples are cooling, pre-heat the oven to 200°C / 400°F / gas mark 6, and grease or line two baking sheets. Once the apples are merely warm, add the peaches and raspberries to them and gently mix together.

4. Roll out your pastry sheets, keeping them on the paper. Using the first sheet, cut six circles, approximately 3½ inches/9cm in diameter – these will be the base of your pies. On the second sheet cut six circles, 4 inches/10cm in diameter – these will be the pie lids.

5. Spoon around 1½ tbsp of the apple, peach and raspberry mix to the centre of the pie bases, making sure to leave at least a clear centimetre around the edges. Then place the lids onto the pies and use a fork to seal the edges together. Finally, take a knife and cut a cross into the tops of the pies to allow the steam to escape. You can also give them a little wash with some melted vegan spread, or soy milk, and dust them with sugar if you wish.

6. Bake in the oven, near the centre, for 10-15 minutes, or until golden brown and the filling is trying to bubble out. Allow to cool before eating – the filling will be perilously hot.

In the home

As I said back in March, I like to do a big clean-out twice a year, and the second one is in September, for that fresh, back-to-school feeling.

It's doubtful (or hopeful) you'll have as much to do this month, and you'll possibly be able to do it thoroughly in a single day, depending on how much you've kept up with it!

To begin, go back through March's list and work through it, paying particular attention to accumulated paperwork, food that's out of date, or will be soon, anything you swore you'd wear again but still haven't, and anything that's accumulated in piles that you haven't found a home for. File everything away so you can find it quickly and easily, and this time be ruthless with things that escaped last time – if you can't use them, it's time to let them go.

The September clean is the best time to set intentions for your home life for the coming six months too; is there anything you'd like to bring into your home? Anything that needs to be replaced, anything that might make your life easier, or lovelier? If you've been collecting stones or mementoes from outside, maybe you could do with somewhere to store or display them. If you've been taking bark rubbings, or drying flowers, perhaps framing and mounting some of your favourites might be a lovely way to bring a little more nature into the home. If you're feeling especially motivated, and you have the time and finances available, why not really lean into the back-to-school feeling by signing up to some classes that allow you to work with natural materials? Willow basket weaving, pottery or floristry might be fun, and will give you a chance to meet new people, learn a new skill, and use nature to create beautiful, functional things. I'm a firm believer in people using their hands to create things – I think a lot of us spend too much time in our heads or on computers and using our hands is a great way to balance that.

And once you've dusted, hoovered and cleaned with the eco-friendly products you've made, change your sheets and pick out fresh pyjamas/loungewear and enjoy your hard-earned autumnal restart. After all, we have a lot of vegetables to eat…

In your phone

With September comes the turn of the season, and so it's time to get back out there with your camera (if you ever stopped) and take more photos of the nature around you.

A particularly fun and interesting thing to do is revisit the spots where you took photos in April, and see how they've changed in the months in between. Note where bare branches grew leaves, then flowers, and now have fruit. Take more photos and compare them, mark the change of the season and the passage of time and the effects it has had.

No matter where you live, and what outdoor space you have access to, you should be able to spot huge differences between then and now – whether that's the amount of foliage on plants, whether berries have replaced flowers, whether ducklings have become ducks, whether butterflies have given way to beetles; the world will have changed in the past five months, and it's important to take a break and acknowledge it.

In caring for yourself

September is a month of change, haunted by the ghost of school-year fresh starts and purposefulness, as well as an innate sense of fun as the autumn festivities begin, and so this month we're going to create something that supports a sense of focus and make a scented room spray.

Scented room soray

10-15 drops of lemon essential oil
10-15 drops of rosemary essential oil
10-15 drops of vetiver essential oil
60ml / 2fl oz / ¼ cup distilled or boiled and cooled water
40ml / 1¼fl oz vodka
A 100ml clean and sterilized spray bottle

Add the essential oils to the bottle and pour the water and vodka inside (the vodka will act as a preserver) and give it a few gentle but firm shakes to mix up the ingredients. Use this spray to fragrance your surroundings whenever you have a task you need to concentrate on – lemon and rosemary are good for creating a sense of calm, decreasing fatigue and promoting focus. Spray some on a piece of cloth to carry around with you if you need a little pep on the go!

In writing

It's likely you'll have heard of **Helen Macdonald** already. Her memoir cum nature writing cum T H White biography **H is for Hawk** was a runaway bestseller and multiple award-winner. *H is for Hawk* documents Macdonald's fostering of a young goshawk in the wake of her father's sudden and unexpected death, and her anger at having such an important part of her life ripped away is mirrored in the young goshawk's fury at being taken from the wild. Alongside it, Macdonald explores the life of T H White, author of *The Once and Future King* quartet.

It's perhaps an unusual choice for us to read: the bringing inside of a wild creature, taking it from the outdoors and raising it in our homes, isn't something I'd advocate, and the motive of this book is to encourage us to get outside a little more! But it is a book about passing seasons, and about noticing the advancement of time, and seeing the world with a quite literal bird's-eye view. The book feels autumnal and golden, and contains some beautiful sections about flying Mabel, the goshawk, and her clear sense of home as she takes to the skies.

I think it serves as a beautiful and moving reminder that nature cannot and should not be contained. The first time I read *H is for Hawk* I wanted nothing so much as a hawk of my own. And the second time I was grateful I didn't have one, and that the bird of my dreams was out there, flying wild and free, as all good things should.

Voices, past and present

September is the month in which the corn dollies are made. They are traditionally crafted at the end of the harvest season, from the last sheaf of corn cut from the fields.

The custom varies county by county (and sometimes village by village!), but the essentials are usually something like this: the last sheaf of corn to be harvested was treated with great care, as it was the refuge of the spirit of the corn – later the goddess of the grain. Rather than using it for food, or milling, it was fashioned into a doll, where the spirit could live over winter.

Because it contained such an important thing to the farmers, it was vital to keep it safe until the season renewed. It was often given pride of place at the Harvest Festival, and treated as an honoured guest, before being kept in the rafters of the farmer's house over winter. It would be burned before the seeds were sown the following year to release the spirit of the goddess, and the ashes ploughed into the earth to ensure a good crop.

Strawcraft has been used in other ways throughout the UK too: given as gifts from men to their sweethearts; or worn to signify the trade of the wearer at trade fairs, with different shapes and additions indicating different roles, such as sheep wool to indicate a shepherd, a plait of horse hair to show a wagoner.

While I was writing this month's almanac section I ordered some straw and made my own dolly to celebrate September in the old way, and if you feel like doing the same there are plenty of videos and suppliers online. My first attempt was challenging, but I'm really pleased with how it turned out (the illustration on page 213 is based on the one I made).

One of the things I like most about the idea of strawcraft is that it offers a chance to make something new and beautiful out of something that might have been abandoned otherwise. Most straw used in modern strawcraft is wheat or rye, and of course it's the seeds that are the most valuable part as they're ground to make flour. The long stalks which form the intricate part of the dollies is either used as bedding for animals or left in the fields to help enrich the soil and prevent soil erosion over winter. I like that taking a few stalks to make the dollies means something new, and unexpected, and beautiful, can be made from it too.

It's the thought of something new and unexpected coming from something that might otherwise be left to perish that made me want to talk to Lizzie Huxley-Jones for the almanac. Though a lot of the people I spoke to while writing this have had a fraught relationship with the outdoors at times, Lizzie is the only one who deliberately turned their back on nature. A non-binary, autistic author from Wales, now based in south London, nature was, at one point, their whole life.

"I grew up in the middle of the countryside, with the mountains at my back and the sea at my feet. And I worked as an ecologist and marine biologist, primarily research diving around places like the Philippines and Honduras. Now I'm an author of children's books, and an editor."

It feels like a huge career jump to me, to go from the ocean being your office to a sitting at a desk, indoors. And it was for Lizzie too; initially an unexpected and unwelcome one at that.

"Nature was my safe space. It was the most obvious thing in the world for me to go into ecology and zoology as a field because I was most at home outside. And it was such an adventure, visiting all these places. I've dived in some of the worst, and best, bodies of water in the world. It wasn't super glamorous, but it was always amazing. Then I got sick."

Lizzie began having seizures. Initially, these were put down to migraines, then as a possible reaction to medication Lizzie was taking at the time. After they stopped taking the medication the seizures seemed to abate, appearing to solve the issue, much to their relief. But then tragedy struck as the seizures returned following a virus, worse than before, forcing Lizzie to hang up their fins.

"I knew I couldn't work with nature the same way anymore, because I couldn't drive, I wouldn't be insured to dive, and it was this sudden, painful thing – the thing I hoped would never happen did, just four years into my career."

Lizzie tried to stay positive and proactive, channelling their love for the ocean into working with charities to promote sustainability in the seafood industries and protect endangered species.

But it wasn't to be. As their health further deteriorated, it became impossible to continue, leaving Lizzie with the devastating realization that the world they'd been part of, and longed for, was lost to them. And having to leave the career and life they loved for a second time was a heartbreak too far.

"Once again, I had to say goodbye, because I was forced to. So I felt this real alienation from nature for quite a few years – to the point where I went to an exhibition about whales at the Natural History Museum and just cried, because I couldn't engage with it, because it wasn't for me anymore."

At the same time, awareness of ocean ecology, thanks to television shows like *Blue Planet*, had gone mainstream, leaving Lizzie – who'd once been an insider – left watching from the sidelines. I asked Lizzie how you could possibly come back from such a monumental loss. How could you possibly heal from such a deep wound?

It started with a dog. For a while, after moving inland, Lizzie and their partner lived with his parents, and there was a beautiful, semi-wild track of land behind their house. As Lizzie began walking Nerys, their dog, every day, they began to notice the natural world around them: plants were flowering, birds were singing in the trees, the seasons were changing the landscape they were coming to know. Against their will, they found the need to learn and engage with nature starting to stir again. But this time Lizzie was cautious, at least to begin with…

"The thing is, when you're a disabled person your access to nature is already constrained, even more so when you're someone who lives in the city. But every day when I can go outside, or I read something, or I garden, it feels like a step further."

It sounds manageable. Sensible too, to gently inch your way back into a world you used to be a native citizen of, and one that has left scars on your heart. But Lizzie understands that nature has very little patience or use for a meandering approach; it favours the hands-on and the bold.

And so they weren't surprised when they found themselves thrown into the deep end once more.

Lizzie was commissioned to write a biography of David Attenborough for children. To their surprise, the more they watched his shows, and researched his initiatives and adventures, the more they found the ache of their own loss was now bearable, and the anger and bitterness at having their dream stolen had become something that could be managed. Lizzie describes it as a big plaster that needed ripping off. And once the plaster was gone, the memories and the love for nature began to return without causing pain.

"Nature was never going to hand out an invitation to return to it. In the natural world, you have to carve out your place, and fight to keep it. So every day is a reclamation."

Like with the corn dollies, Lizzie has taken something that seemed unusable and is weaving something beautiful from it. It's a design for life we could all consider a little more. There might be treasures in the dirt if we're willing to look for them.

September

In your hands

October

Regarding October

All hail October, the spookiest month of the year! Autumn is most definitely here now. I'm sure you'll have noticed the smell of smoke in the air even if you live miles from anywhere with open fires; just tilt your nose to the sky, inhale and it'll be there, a hint of char and ash and then gone. The nights close in fast, lights are turned on earlier, curtains are closed. Big coats will have come out of storage (check your pockets and see if your past self left you a present!), scarves and hats will be retrieved, there will be a panic when you can only find one glove – relax, the other is there (though it's unlikely to turn up before you buy a replacement pair). Sandals and shoes will be giving way to old familiar boots, or new ones that need to be worn in.

If you get outside this month, you'll be able to kick, wander or wheel your way through piles of fallen leaves. Everything will have taken on shades of ochre, orange and brown. When the sun shines the world will seem gilded, and when it doesn't it might seem glum, but it isn't. It's the natural cycle of things, and those dull browns and yellows are an essential part of that. Those colours mean recycling and rejuvenation, the slow decay of leaves into the soil, where worms will munch on them and turn them into delicious nutrients plants will use the following spring. Nothing in nature is ever wasted; everything has a purpose.

There are still a few things left to forage – haws, the last of the damsons, some nuts – but mostly these days nature's pantry is bare, and it's kinder to leave things you see now for the animals and birds that will need them.

It's an exciting month for mushrooms, though! In October, fairy-tale favourite the fly agaric is king; the red cap with white spots is unmistakeable, though it's also poisonous. Fly agaric is most commonly found near silver birch trees, and while you're there you should look up to check for the birch polypore on the trunk, too. Common puffballs and amethyst deceivers are also around, along with the turkey tail bracket fungus and the very common and also deadly brown roll-rim. As with everything, check, check and check again before you touch, and always consult an expert if there's any doubt.

If you live near an area with red deer, or mule deer in the west of the US, white-tailed deer in the east, it's well worth trying to get out, especially early in the morning, to hear and maybe even see them rutting. I never have and I desperately want to; apparently the bellow of a red stag warning others to stay the hell away or else is really something! Animal activity is a little slower; their thoughts are turning to their winter homes and it's natural yours would be too.

Just make sure you do keep getting outside if and when you can; even though things are slower, they haven't stopped, and the natural spaces around you will keep changing. As ever, if you can't, keep an eye on those feeds and catch up with any friends or acquaintances you've made online through your journey. Compare notes!

If you are going to go outside, don't go out on All Hallows' Eve – traditionally it's the time of year the boundary between our world and the other world is the thinnest, and you never know what's lurking on the other side of the veil. Maybe this one time it's better to stay at home, to light a candle to ward off the dark, eat good soup and drink warming drinks and indulge in a good old-fashioned ghost story.

In the skies

Our first celestial event is one of two meteor showers this month. **The Draconids** is the smaller of the two, peaking on **7 October.** The moon will be slightly too bright to see all but the most powerful, but if you're eager to try, find the constellation Draco and watch for them radiating out from there.

On the **8th, Mercury reaches its greatest western elongation**, and gives us a final opportunity to see it in 2022. Look to the eastern horizon early in the morning to spot it.

The **Hunter's Moon rises at 20:54 GMT on 9 October,** named for the time of year that game was at its fattest, ready to face winter, and so the best time for the hunters to gather the food they'd need to survive the cold and dark months.

The **21st and 22nd herald the peak of the Orionids,** with around 20 meteors per hour radiating out from Orion. The Orionids are the product of Halley's Comet – possibly the most famous comet in the world. Though the comet only comes into Earth's vicinity every 75 years, with the next opportunity to see it being 2061, the Orionids happen annually, so we can see a little legendary stardust every year if we choose to.

The **new moon occurs at 10:48 GMT on the 25th,** and there will also be a partial solar eclipse on the same day. We won't see much of it in the UK, but those in central Russia will have an excellent view.

Check List:

☐
☐
☐
☐
☐
☐
☐
☐

In the soil

PLANTS YOU CAN SOW THIS MONTH:
Herbs indoors, if you have the light
and heat available for them.

MAINTENANCE THIS MONTH: Keep an
eye on your herbs and any salad
leaves you still have. There's not
much else really, just keep them
ticking over. You've done so well this
year. I hope you're proud of yourself.
And it's not too early to start thinking
about what you might grow next year.
Maybe if you seriously caught the
growing bug you'll even look into
local allotments and put your name
on a waiting list. Plots can come
around faster than you think.

HARVESTING THIS MONTH: Basil,
chives, rosemary, mint, late radishes.

In season

There's still a lot of fresh and seasonal food to be found in October. **Apples, bilberries, blackberries, elderberries, medlars, pears, figs** and **grapes** are still in season. **Quinces** are now around too.

As far as veg go, we still have **artichokes, beetroot (beets), broccoli, runner beans, fennel, kale, kohlrabi, leeks, lettuce, marrow, mushrooms, potatoes, pumpkin, radishes, rocket, shallots, sweetcorn, marrow, tomatoes** and **turnips. Butternut squash, celeriac** and **salsify** are in season; **parsnips** and **chicory** are back too.

If you're like me, more than anything you'll associate October with pumpkins. Thanks, in part, to a certain coffee chain, the prevalence of pumpkin-flavoured things has exploded over the past few years, and so where once our pumpkin options might have been a can of pumpkin puree in the world food aisle or a giant beast bred for carving instead of flavour, we now have options, even if we haven't grown our own. So we're going to take advantage of that, and make a creamy pumpkin risotto. Risotto is one of my favourite things to make and eat, a little because it's so versatile and you can make enough to last a few days, and also because it's something I can eat with a spoon, which means I can read at the same time.

Pumpkin risotto

Ingredients

250g / 9oz fresh pumpkin, peeled and cut into 1-inch chunks

1 tbsp of Olive oil

Salt and pepper, to taste (but be wary of using salt if adding the miso)

2 tsp dried sage

1 white onion, diced

1 tbsp vegan butter

3 cloves garlic, crushed

1 tsp dried cumin

150g / 5½ oz Arborio or carnaroli rice

80ml / 2½fl oz / ⅓ cup dry white wine

2 pints / 1.1 litre / 5 cups vegetable stock

1 tsp white miso paste (optional)

2 heaped tbsp nutritional yeast

Method

1. Preheat the oven to 200°C / 400°F / gas mark 6. Place the chopped pumpkin on a baking sheet and liberally douse it in olive oil, dried sage, salt and pepper and roast for 30 minutes.

2. While the pumpkin cooks, sauté the chopped onion in the vegan butter, using a large pan or wok, until it's soft, but not brown. Then add the crushed garlic, cumin and the rice to the pan and cook with the buttery onions for 1 minute, before adding the wine and stirring it in.

3. Then it's time to begin adding the stock, 250ml at a time, stirring all the while. Add the miso if you're using it, too.

4. Keep doing this, and adding stock as the risotto thickens and absorbs it, which usually takes 15–20 minutes. If you use all the stock and the rice still isn't cooked to your preference, then add hot water in small increments until you're happy.

5. Remove from the heat and stir in the nutritional yeast until it's part of the risotto. Remove your pumpkin from the oven and add it to the risotto, oil and all.

I like to top mine off with Violife Greek Block, which doesn't taste anything like a hard Greek cheese to me, but does remind me a lot of a soft goats' cheese, and so pairs incredibly well with the pumpkin and the sage.

In the home

We're now in the thick of autumn, the time of year when, at least for appearance's sake, the natural world is shutting up shop and slowing down. But it's also a time of rich, earthy colours, so what can we find outside to help make our homes feel more connected?

- Pine cones can be cleaned, dried and painted – my nana used to do this, spraying them silver and gold and attaching string to them to make festive decorations. I think they're just as pretty left in their natural state, or with just the edges painted in your favourite colour.

- Berries we can dry to create garlands with (please make sure you don't pick anything poisonous – use the app you downloaded in February to help you identify them!).

- If there are acorns still around then they're a fun and sweet item to collect, too!

- Dried leaves can be used to make table centrepieces or wreaths for doors; pine cones, dried berries and fruits can also be added.

- Dried leaves can also be decoupaged to make greetings cards or gift labels.

- If you made a coaster or dish in summer, why not repeat the process to make a matching autumnal counterpart?

- Or get even craftier – buy fabric paint and paint the leaves, then press the design onto T-shirts, napkins, handkerchiefs, cushion covers, or anything else you feel like! Just remember to heat-seal the paint if you don't want it to wash out.

Check List:

☐
☐
☐
☐
☐
☐
☐
☐

Check List:

- [ ]
- [ ]
- [ ]
- [ ]
- [ ]
- [ ]
- [ ]
- [ ]

In your phone

I promised you in February the technology clean-out would have a second act, and this is it. If you made a list back then, now is the time to revisit it and make some final decisions on all those apps, files, people, and anything else you were hesitating about. If in the last nine months you haven't used them, or haven't reached out, let them go – if for no other reason than to free up some storage space you can use for something else! Take the chance too to go through anything you've added since that might not be serving you as well as you'd hoped – maybe the plant-identifying app and the breathing apps you've tried didn't catch your interest; if so, say goodbye to them.

In caring for yourself

This is an indulgent soak designed for sorceresses. It can be used in a regular bath for a luxurious soak, or, if you don't have access to a full-size bath, or don't like taking baths, it can also be used in a footbath (or repurposed washing-up bowl, to be realistic). Either way, you'll want to make sure you have a nice, fluffy towel, your favourite moisturizer, and something cozy to wear for afterwards.

Homemade bath soak

100g / 3½oz raw shea butter

2 tbsp sweet almond oil / coconut oil (unless you use a scentless coconut oil, the final product will smell coconutty, so bear that in mind when you're choosing your essential oils!)

Dried flowers (I like lavender, but roses, marigolds or whatever you want will work)

A few drops of your favourite essential oil (I use bergamot, but to each their own)

50g / 1¾oz oats

1 tbsp lemon juice

A square of cheesecloth, around 20cm x 20cm

A ramekin, ideally with sloped sides. A cup will work too!

Break up the shea butter into chunks and place in a heatproof bowl, inside a pan of simmering water. Allow it to melt. Add the sweet almond/coconut oil to the shea butter and stir in. Then add the flowers, and the essential oil. Finally, stir in the oats. Carefully remove the bowl from the heat and set aside, allowing it to cool for 10 or so minutes. In the meantime, line your ramekin / cup with the cheesecloth, making sure the sides are all of an even height. Pour the melted butter mix into the ramekin / cup, and place in the fridge until it sets. Once it has set, gently pull it out of the ramekin / cup and tie all the sides together in a knot.

You can then throw this in your bath / footbath and allow it to melt, infusing the water with oils and scents. It will also keep in the fridge for a couple of weeks if you don't want to use it straight away!

In writing

Earlier in the almanac we met **Kiran Millwood Hargrave**, who spoke to us about wild swimming and how nature has worked alongside traditional therapy and prescribed medication to help her manage her depression, and October's book is by her. **The Mercies** is Kiran's first adult fiction novel, and it tells a fictionalized version of the events in the Norwegian island of Vardø in 1617, when the witch hunters came to town.

What follows is a tale of love, loss and longing stitched through with fear and oppression, in a town where nature has suddenly and brutally wiped out the vast majority of the male population, leaving the women to pick up the pieces. The same year, laws against witchcraft are passed, initially to suppress the Sami people in the very north of Finnmark, as was, but they're quickly, and typically, used against any women who are seen as unnatural and suspicious. And what could be more suspicious than an island full of women who have taken on the entirety of the work the island needs to survive, including wearing men's clothes for some of the tasks.

I chose it for this month partially because it's October, and it's a story about witches – or what men think witches are. But mostly because it's about women learning the land they live upon, and working with nature in a way they weren't usually permitted to. Like *Circe* in August, these women find themselves after the very worst has happened, and the way they do it is by opening their hearts and minds to nature, and the natural energies around them. It's a theme every book I've chosen has at its core: learning to be open to the earth.

Voices, past and present

I can't talk about October without talking about Halloween, and I thought this month it would be fun to share some traditional spells that were performed on the night when the veil between worlds is thinnest, for anyone feeling brave or curious enough to try them out. A lot of Halloween spells seem to centre on love, which might be surprising until you consider that there are still a lot of cold and dark days to go before spring, and so the daydream of a grand passion might be just what's needed to get you through the winter months.

If you're single (or ambitious) and would like to discover the identity of your future spouse, why not make a Dumb Cake? My favourite version of this ritual was told to me by my nana and it goes like this:

On All Hallows' Eve, before midnight, you must make a cake in complete silence. You can't utter a single sound. The cake should be made from wheat flour, barley flour and water, added in equal amounts to make a thick dough. Salt should be added too, and the mixture baked with the doors of the house open to let the smell out, to entice your future groom/bride to the house. Before midnight, you must cut two slices from the cake, and lay them out, carving your initials into one and leaving the other blank, and the knife beside it. Then you must walk backwards to your bed, and get into it, still remaining silent. If you're to be married within the year, you'll see your suitor following you up the stairs to bed, and you must not let them catch you or else they'll be untrue during your marriage. If you don't see them, check the second slice of cake in the morning and you might find a pair of initials in it – that's your man/woman. If you don't see anything, that means they didn't come, so you have to try again.

Alternatively, as midnight approaches, peel an apple in one go, then toss the single piece of peel over your shoulder. The shape should form the initial of the one you're going to marry.

One final option is to wash a cloth in a stream, or some running water, and hang it up to dry. As midnight approaches, gaze into the cloth and you might see the face of your intended staring back out at you.

A practising witch and author, Anna McKerrow writes about witches, the natural world and healing in a variety of different guises, and in her own life she relates to nature as a sacred, special thing; her own spiritual practices and beliefs centre around elemental energies and natural forces.

"I feel strong connections to the earth and its power places in particular, and relate to nature as sacred. I don't consider it as external to me," Anna tells me. "I take a holistic 'everything is me, and I am everything' life view, and that includes nature, society and other people too. So I am connected to everything and part of the whole."

She goes on to describe how difficult the "everything is me, and I am everything" ethos can be to reconcile with her ego when she comes across views and behaviours of things she doesn't like or agree with. But she works to accept that nature isn't moral and it's important to understand that.

"A pagan, pantheistic worldview means that I think of events in my life or in the world at large as part of a cyclic model of energies – life/death/rebirth, waxing and waning lunar energies and seasons. It also means that I consider myself to have a personal, direct and unmediated (i.e. without the need for a priest, etc. to intercede on my behalf) relationship with nature as personified by deities, particularly Pan, Babalon and Aphrodite, which is illuminating. The deities are very real presences."

Unlike many of the interviewees, and myself, Anna has found her relationship with nature is something that's developed as she's grown older.

"One daily connection to nature I do in this way is the Lesser Banishing Ritual of the Pentagram, which sounds worryingly occult, but in fact it's like a five-minute daily meditation (you can find lots of videos online of people demonstrating it in a variety of witchy and non-witchy ways; it doesn't matter which version you like, it's all the same). In doing it, you intone the names of the angels associated with north, south, east and west, connect to their energies, and situate yourself in the centre of all being with your body as a cardinal cross at the middle of everything. I'm also lucky enough to have a garden so I like to grow vegetables and fruit and work in the garden as much as I can. It's very calming and grounding. If I have a problem with a book I can't work out, I weed the garden as a kind of physical un-knotting of the problem, which usually works, and also means I do the weeding."

Until her twenties she thought of herself as a bookish, indoors person, but as she's aged she's found a love of the outdoors, to the point she's now the one chivvying her husband and son to get out and get some fresh air. The benefits of it to Anna are clear.

"Fresh air! Exercise! All that has a positive effect on mood. Humans are supposed to be outside people. Not supposed to be cooped up indoors. There's that research about the positive ions produced by walking barefoot outdoors, isn't

there? People assume it's an airy-fairy idea, but it's scientific fact that making direct connection with the earth is good for you. Same with the air at the seaside; we used to think it was a 'tonic' like an old wives' tale, but now we know that there are good reasons why sea air is good for you."

Like so many of us, she's also found it beneficial to her mental state, and here she circles back to her opening remarks, about accepting nature as simply something that "is", rather than something good, or bad, or moral in any way. "Being accepting of nature's shadow is quite liberating. Looking at nature and the changing of the seasons is one of the most easily profound ways of really understanding this on a visceral level."

October

In your hands

November

Regarding November

I love the last four months of the year best of all. I love the coziness of them, the way they demand blankets and jumpers and thick socks to combat the chill, but also the air of festivity throughout too. From the harvest and the equinox in September, Halloween in October, Guy Fawkes Night on the 5th of this month (I will tolerate well-organized and well-marshalled displays) and, in the United States, Thanksgiving toward the end of November, before the biggest party season of them all. I like that we have taken these months of darkness and coldness and turned them into times of light and celebration – I think that's the best of us.

It's possible now, depending on your daily lives, that you can only comfortably get outside at the weekends, and that's determined by the weather, but I'd urge you to do it, even if it's just a brisk march around a park on a Sunday afternoon. Once you're out, you might as well stay out for a bit longer and see what you can see. And if you can't then it's time to join your housebound colleagues in watching the webcams. If possible, reach out online and see if any of them have advice or tips for you that they're willing to share (but please remember they're not obliged to help you navigate an unfamiliar world and be grateful for any help you are given).

Look to the skies or screens for starling murmurations! During winter thousands of them fly to Britain and create the most mesmerizing and sensational aerial displays! As the sun begins to set, they take flight, joined by hundreds and thousands of others, and create the most incredible shapes, ducking and weaving, the motion rippling through the flock like a wave. It ends as suddenly as it starts, some secret signal given, and then they dive for their roosts, leaving onlookers feeling a little dizzy. I have a soft spot for starlings – I think they're incredibly beautiful, and I was once told that to other birds they're dazzling. Birds are tetrachromats, meaning that while they see the three colours we trichromats (humans and other primates) see, they can also see UV. So it's possible (based on what we know about human vision) that starlings' already lovely iridescent feathers appear completely different to birds, startlingly bright and luminous – look it up! I also

have a soft spot for magpies too. I think they're great and you should too.

Other things to spot this month are more mushrooms, and there are some really wild examples out there. It's worth getting an app or guidebook and looking for them; some of the stranger ones include dead man's fingers, candlesnuff fungus, and wood blewit, which are sometimes a lovely purple colour.

If you live near a river known to host salmon, go and have a look for them! It's in November that they swim inland and travel upstream to lay their eggs. Every year they face such a struggle just to get to where they're going, but they keep trying. They keep trying.

In the skies

The **4th and 5th of November is the peak of the Taurids** meteor shower. Though it actually begins in September, it's the result of debris from two different **comets**, the unromantically named **2P/Encke** and **asteroid 2004 TG10**. And with the arrival of the **Beaver Moon at 11:02 GMT on 8 November,** only the brightest meteors will be visible if the weather is clear. But fear not, because there are more meteor showers to come.

The **total lunar eclipse is on 8 November,** giving us the year's second, and final, blood moon (the same term is used to apply to the four eclipses in a row, which is not the case this time).

The following day, on the **9th, we have a chance to see Uranus at opposition to the sun,** as a tiny blue-green dot in the night sky.

The **17th–18th is the peak of the Leonids meteor shower,** radiating out from – you guessed it – the constellation of Leo, with an average of 15 meteors per hour. The Leonids are unusual, as every 33 years they have a kind of super-meteor event, where hundreds of meteors can be seen every hour at the peak. Sadly, the next one won't be until 2034.

And finally for November, the **new moon occurs at 22:57 GMT on the 23rd.**

Check List:

- [ ]
- [ ]
- [ ]
- [ ]
- [ ]
- [ ]
- [ ]
- [ ]

In the soil

PLANTS YOU CAN SOW THIS MONTH:
Herbs indoors, if you have the light
and heat available for them.

MAINTENANCE THIS MONTH: Keep an
eye on your herbs and any salad leaves
you still have. There's not much else
really, just keep them ticking over and
keep dreaming of the things you'll
grow when the wheel turns and spring
comes again.

HARVESTING THIS MONTH: Indoor
basil, chives, rosemary, mint, spinach.

In season

Citrus fruits begin to make a reappearance in November: starting with **clementines** and **satsumas**, and **passionfruits** and **pomegranates** return too. **Apples**, **quinces** and **pears** are still available, and **cranberries** are now in season, for those wanting to make an early jump on cranberry sauce.

There are still lots of fresh vegetables to be had, too. **Artichoke**, **beetroot (beets)**, **butternut squash**, **celeriac**, **celery**, **chicory**, **kale**, **kohlrabi**, **leeks**, **mushrooms**, **parsnips**, **potatoes**, **pumpkin**, **salsify** and **turnips** remain seasonal treasures. They're joined by **swede (rutabaga)** and **cauliflower**, both making their way back to our tables for the winter months.

I am someone who loves creamy, buttery dishes best of all. I love a rich, velvety sauce; I love the decadence of it, and how luxurious and smooth it tastes. I especially love it in November, when the weather has turned and our hearts and minds start wanting cozy, warm things again: blankets and cushions and candles and things that fill us up and make us feel grounded and full. So, for November's recipe I've paired seasonal earthy mushrooms with a creamy sauce to make a rustic and late-autumnal-feeling mushroom fricassee.

Mushroom fricassee

Ingredients

2 tbsp vegan spread

1 medium shallot / white onion, finely chopped

1 carrot, sliced into 2cm chunks (don't make them perfect!)

2 garlic cloves, crushed

Salt and pepper, to taste

1 tbsp dried tarragon

250g/9 oz mixed mushrooms, thickly sliced. I like to use fresh chestnut, button and Portobello (which are really all the same mushroom at different stages of growth) along with dried oyster, porcini and shitake. If you use dried mushrooms, please remember to rehydrate them before cooking, and to save the liquid, as you can use it in the sauce.

80ml / 2½fl oz / ⅓ cup dry white wine

1 tbsp cornstarch

300ml / 10½fl oz vegetable stock (make your rehydrated mushroom water part of this if you use them)

100ml / 3½fl oz / scant ½ cup vegan cream substitute / coconut milk (the thick white part) (Please bear in mind that if you use coconut milk, the finished fricassee will retain the flavour!)

Method

1. On a medium heat, add 2 tbsp vegan spread to a large wok / pan and melt, then add the onions and carrots and gently sauté until they're soft - don't let them crisp or turn too brown. When the onions are translucent, add the garlic, salt, pepper and tarragon and cook for one minute, stirring to keep the garlic from browning.

2. Then add the mushrooms and wine and cook for 5 minutes. The mushrooms should begin to sweat and form a rich gravy in the pan.

3. Add the cornstarch to the mushroom gravy until it absorbs all of the liquid. Then begin to add the stock, a little at a time, stirring at it reduces and thickens. Add the vegan / coconut cream and cook for a further 5 minutes, or until the sauce is a thick, caramel brown.

You can serve it with rice, crusty bread, polenta, pasta or potatoes – whatever you feel like on the day!

In the home

With the outside world turning dark and cold once more, you might find you start to miss the greenery of spring and summer, especially now you've (hopefully) been spending so much time in it. Plants have been proven to have a hugely beneficial influence on mood; according to the RHS website at the time of writing, houseplants have a number of physiological and psychological effects on us, including:

- Improving mood
- Reducing stress levels
- Increasing productivity
- Reducing blood pressure

One study even found they reduced headaches and fatigue by 20–25%!

And that's aside from how they brighten up dark corners and provide something lovely and fresh for us to look at and care for.

It's highly likely you have one, or many, houseplants already, and if so take this month as a reminder to cherish them. Make sure they're not root-bound, dust off any waxy leaves, prune them if necessary, and cut away any dead or dying foliage or plants. Maybe even invest in some pretty new pots for them, or use air-drying or oven-drying clay to make your own if you're feeling adventurous.

On the off-chance you don't own a plant, or you do but

it's a cactus or succulent you've had forever and you're not entirely sure how it's still alive, then maybe it's time to get yourself a new friend.

Here are some of my favourite, easy-to-care-for plants:

Pilea peperomioides, also known as a Chinese Money Plant or Pancake Plant (or, if you're me, a Pepperoni Plant), is a fun, evergreen plant that grows fairly large, round, pancake/pepperoni-style leaves on long stems that fan out from a long, central stalk. It likes sunlight, sandy, well-drained soil, and if you keep it happy it will have an  astonishing amount of "pups" – Pilea babies, which will grow from the main plant. You can cut them free with a very sharp and sterile knife once they get 2–3 inches tall, and then put them into water or soil to root. Mine started having pups after a year and at the time of writing I have seven transplanted and it's got another five on the go. Another lovely nickname for the Pilea is the Pass-it-on plant, for this very prolific reason!

African violets are beloved of a certain generation of women, and rightly so, because under the right circumstances they will bloom continuously, and they're easily propagated from a leaf carefully cut away and planted in soil. It'll take a few months, but eventually a new plant will grow. The blooms come in a variety of colours, whites through pink and lilac to deepest violet, and it's a cheery classic. They only like to be watered from the bottom – never get the leaves wet! They also prefer being a little bit root-bound, and like sunlight, but not too much – filtered through a curtain is ideal for them.

Peace lilies are stalwart houseplants, famed for cleaning the air around them, at least according to a study by NASA (please bear in mind the research was conducted on space stations, which have an artificial and controlled environment and so it's unlikely the effect will be the same in your home!). Even if they don't, when they're happy they grow tall and lush with rich green leaves and long, tall white flowers. It's happy in the shade, and only needs to be watered at most once a week. It much prefers dry soil to wet, so will survive gentle neglect! It will need dusting though.

One final note is to please remember to consider the plants you'd like carefully if you live in a home with pets. What's harmless to us can be fatal to animals, so do your research first.

In your phone

Following on from the clean-out, and in the spirit of it almost being the holiday season for a lot of the Western world, use November to reach out again. December is usually a busy month for everyone, winding up the year and getting ready for the festivities to come, so November is the perfect time to check in on people – maybe the people you last spoke to in June, or maybe others who've slipped away a little in the interim months. Take a few moments to send messages, or like and comment on old pictures or posts, reply to emails. The year as we mark it is almost over; it's time to wish everyone well with what comes next.

In caring for yourself

As the weather starts to turn, our skin will need a little extra care and attention to keep it happy. So this month we're going to make a banana oat mask to soothe our skin after it's been exposed to the cold and wet weather outside.

Banana oat mask

Pin or tie your hair back, and clean your skin in your usual manner.

In a clean bowl, mash a banana until it's a good, thick pulp, then add 2 tbsp of oatmeal (you can easily make your own by crushing rolled oats with a pestle and mortar). Then add either 1 tbsp of oat milk or 1 tsp of coconut oil, depending on your skin type – if your skin is oily or prone to acne, use the milk; if it's normal, try the coconut oil – and mix all of the ingredients together thoroughly, then apply to the face in an even layer, avoiding the mouth and eyes.

Lie down with a towel under your head (the mixture will slide, and it's messy!) and leave the mask on for 5–10 minutes, before rinsing with lukewarm (not hot) water until your face is clean. If you're feeling very bold, splash your face after with cold water and pat (not rub) dry with a towel, or an old T-shirt.

In writing

This month I've chosen **Josie George's** extraordinary memoir, ***A Still Life***. In January 2018, Josie set out to record a year of her life, and the changing of the seasons, but the most remarkable thing about it is that Josie is chronically ill and has been since childhood; most of what she experiences happens within a very close radius of her terraced house in the West Midlands, and a lot of her interactions with and observations of nature happen from inside that home, through her window. And yet *A Still Life* is one of the broadest, most open and curious books I've ever read. Her experiences of nature and the world around her are intimate and intricate; because she doesn't have the ability to climb mountains or swim rivers, she finds magic and wonder in the things most of us don't value: the patterns of ice in puddles, the urban birds that make their home in her neighbourhood.

Josie has an incredible gift for making the most mundane things seem magical, for wringing out the joy and wonder from every possible thing, and for making the most of what she has – and yet she's no Pollyanna; she's open and explicit about the struggles she faces and the limitations and effects of her illnesses on her life, and on those of her family. She doesn't slap a brave face on it to make it easier for us to read. Rather she lives, as fully and as often as she can, learning to listen to the rhythm of her body while she observes and delights in the world around her. It's a glorious, uplifting treasure of a book, and will warm the cockles of your heart through all the dark nights of November. Josie is proof that you don't need to live in a thatched cottage in the countryside, or on the edge of a vast moorland, to appreciate and marvel at the natural world around you. There is nature everywhere, in everything, and it's all magnificent and wondrous.

Voices, past and present

As a child, I was absolutely fascinated by the Cottingley Fairies, and read every single thing about them I could get my hands on. The idea that real fairies would appear to two girls in Yorkshire and allow themselves to be photographed, and the fact that dozens of experts and figures of the day, including Arthur Conan Doyle, could find no evidence of forgery or trickery in the photos, lit up my mind like nothing else. I still have Conan Doyle's book, **The Coming of the Fairies**, and it continues to delight me that this man of science and reason – who wrote the most famous detective in the world, who sees through all subterfuge and trickery – could believe in fairies.

When I was young I wanted so badly for fairies – and if not fairies then ghosts or vampires or anything mythical or magical – to be real. I looked for them all the time, especially through the winter months, between Halloween and Midwinter's Day, convinced if it was going to happen it would be then, when everything between the real world and the Otherworld was a bit muddled.

I was so disappointed when I found out the cousins who had supposedly been the centre of the fairies' attention confessed they'd made it all up, and fabricated the images using paper cutouts of fairies, painted by one of the girls.

All except one. The fifth and final photo, which Frances Griffiths, the younger of the cousins, claimed until the day she died was real, and that there really had been fairies in the garden.

The story of the Cottingley Fairies is a testament to the imaginative powers of young girls to believe in the impossible. But while Frances and Elsie manifested fairies, November's Voice, Katie Marsden, manifested a different kind of life. She recalls being eight, or maybe nine, and coming across a battered cardboard house full of herb seeds at a jumble sale and buying it, convinced she could coax growth from them. And she did. She grew basil, coriander (cilantro) and parsley and, encouraged, her parents gave her a patch of garden and she kept growing, specializing in herbs at first and then as she grew up expanding her repertoire to include chillies, which she pollinated with a paintbrush.

It's fair to say Katie has always been a gardener, though her route to embracing it as an adult has taken her via a few unexpected detours. She used to work in radio, as a producer of comedy programming, a job that she loved but didn't believe was where her long-term future lay. So she began studying for the RHS qualifications that would help to make her dream of being a professional horticulturalist a reality.

But it was not to be. First her plan was (happily) interrupted by the birth of her daughter, and then again, this time unhappily by a deterioration in her health.

Unbeknownst to her until symptoms began to show, Katie was born with a joint condition that progressively hampered her ability to spend long periods of time doing intensely physical work – the mainstay of working as a gardener. So, with her professional dreams now out of reach, she turned instead to home gardening, and cultivating a variety of plants in the garden of her rented home; for eating, to support local wildlife, for scent, and for general enjoyment and appreciation.

Luckily, Katie grew up in what she calls a "garden-y family".

"My granddad grew a lot of vegetables, and so did my dad, and my mum is a plant-lover too, though her approach is less structured than theirs. Because of where I grew up, we had a big garden, and it was quite ahead of its time, I suppose, because a lot of it was wild, really, really wild, and it was left like that for the wildlife. We had badgers in the garden, and owls, and frogs and newts."

These days, she's continuing the family tradition of cultivating and growing, and in addition to a garden she has an allotment, though her health can make it difficult to maintain and she's figuring out how to make it work for her.

"It's important to me, though," she tells me. "Putting roots in soil. I have to do it. I have to find a way."

Katie finds peace, even sanity, in growing. At numerous points while we chat, she mentions that gardening is a touchstone for her in terms of managing her mental health, and how it's become even more important to her as her physical health has presented challenges. Gardening offers her a chance to stay active, but it's a satisfying kind of activity, not as arbitrary as conventional exercise, but a way to keep moving and, most importantly for her, a way to connect with the element that gives her both joy and peace. "I struggle if I can't find a way to get soil on my hands," she says.

I ask her if she has any advice to offer to anyone who is new to gardening, and her reply makes me laugh.

"I am an orchid murderer," she breezes. "I think people think that people who are green-fingered don't ever kill anything, but they do. If you kill a lot of plants, it doesn't mean you're bad at it – a lot of plants are terribly hard to look after. Don't base your ideas of how to succeed on what other people are growing, and don't be afraid to find the bits of gardening that you love. If you love carnivorous plants and hate roses, that's fine."

November

In your hands

December

Regarding December

We're almost at the end of another year, and by now we should be feeling quite comfortable outside – maybe we're even dressing for it. A common saying in Scandinavia, and Scotland, is that there's no such thing as bad weather, only unsuitable clothing, and I believe in it. There are very few meteorological events that can't be mitigated by a good raincoat, a jumper, some wellies and – if you really want to get serious – waterproof trousers. But if you're sticking to local parks and small woodlands, you might not think they're necessary, and you're right.

December is, for me, a simultaneously quiet and loud month. The loudness is obvious and comes from humans: the joy of seeing people you love, of choosing things to please them, of coming together to share food and drink. It's a social time of year for Homo sapiens, and a bright spot to combat the winter equinox, when the sun spends the least amount of time above the horizon, and the further north you live the more you'll be aware of this.

But it's also a quieter time too. So much of the natural world is sleeping. Hedgehogs have gone to ground, dormice and bats too; badgers don't hibernate, but they do try to sleep and conserve as much energy as they can, only venturing out when it's mild. Snakes enter brumation, a kind of hibernation for cold-blooded creatures, along with frogs and toads, limiting as much of their bodily functions as they can to conserve energy. Foxes still abound, in fact December is the beginning of their mating season, and so it's pretty common to hear the three barks followed by a scream that is their signature cry at this time of year.

Make sure you take a few moments to be quiet too, and recalibrate yourself with nature. Take a solo walk early on a wintry afternoon, checking in on all of the places that have become so familiar, and maybe even loved, throughout the year. Or wrap up warm and open a window. Steal a moment to pause and close your eyes, turning your face to the weak sun, breathing in cold, clean air. Pause to listen to the wind through bare branches, the songs of the birds who make their homes here all year round. You're part of this now, this world of outside, this place where everything works together in harmony, and everything has a role to play. You have a role to play in it too. Whether that's protector and defender, educator, grower, or just appreciator, you're connected now. What a brilliant thing.

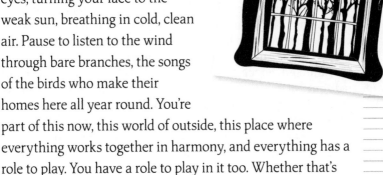

In the skies

December 2022 is a hugely busy month in the skies! Beginning on the 8th at 04:08 GMT, we have the Cold Moon, and Mars at opposition to the sun on the same night. It will be very bright, easily spotted as the reddish orange unblinking spot in the sky.

Then the Geminids meteor shower, peaking over the 13th and 14th. It is the most popular meteor shower, because at its peak you can expect to see up to 120 meteors per hour, meaning you shouldn't have to stay out in the cold December air for too long to see something. The light from the waning Cold Moon will block out the fainter ones, but there should be plenty more to see. Find Gemini and watch for them radiating out from there.

A trifecta of celestial brilliance can be seen on the 21st. Mercury is at its greatest eastern elongation again (gotta love those small-orbit planets), so if you missed viewing it in August, here is a second chance, low in the western sky after sunset.

The 21st is also the peak of the Ursids meteor shower. It's a small shower, with only five to ten meteors per hour, but if the skies are clear and you're away from light pollution it will be dark enough to see them – best of all just after midnight. Do wrap up warm, though.

Most importantly, the 21st is the winter solstice at 21:48 GMT. Dark sister to June's summer solstice, it's the day of the year when the hours of night are at their maximum, and marks the first day of winter in the northern hemisphere.

Finally, our last new moon occurs at 10:16 GMT on the 23rd, making the festive season the perfect time to start planting new seeds and ideas for 2023.

In the soil

PLANTS YOU CAN SOW THIS MONTH: Herbs indoors, if you have the light and heat available for them.

MAINTENANCE THIS MONTH: Keep an eye on your herbs and any salad leaves you still have. There's not much else really, just keep them ticking over and keep dreaming of the things you'll grow when the wheel turns and spring comes again.

HARVESTING THIS MONTH: Indoor basil, chives, rosemary, mint, spinach.

In season

Pineapples are back! They always seem to me like such a summery fruit, but in fact they're most readily available in winter in the UK. Also available are **apples** and **pears**, **clementines**, **cranberries**, **pomegranates**, **satsumas** and **tangerines**. All that Vitamin C just in time for winter. **Passionfruits** are now in season too.

And on the more savoury side of produce, **beetroot (beets)**, **cauliflower**, **celeriac**, **celery**, **chicory**, **kale**, **kohlrabi**, **leeks**, **mushrooms**, **parsnips**, **potatoes**, **salsify**, **shallots**, **swede (rutabaga)** and, you guessed it, **turnips** are still in season. Welcome back to **Brussels sprouts** and **Jerusalem artichokes**, too.

Year's end cassoulet

Ingredients

2 tbsp olive oil

1 white onion, chopped

250g / 9oz parsnips, chopped into 1-inch chunks

1 tsp dried marjoram

2 garlic cloves, crushed

1 x 400g / 14oz can butter beans or 180g / 7oz dried butter beans, soaked in water for at least 12 hours before using (the volume will then double to 360g, matching the drained weight of the canned beans)

1 x 400g / 14oz can chopped tomatoes

200ml / 7fl oz / 1 scant cup vegetable stock

80ml / 2½fl oz / ⅓ cup red wine

Salt and pepper, to taste

Method

1. Preheat your oven to 180°C / 350°F / gas mark 4.

2. In a wok or large pan on the hob, heat your oil and add the chopped onions. Fry gently until just beginning to turn gold, then add the parsnips, marjoram and garlic and cook for another 5 minutes, stirring to keep the browning even and to stop the marjoram burning.
3. Add the beans, tomatoes, stock and wine. Bring to the boil, then transfer into an oven-safe dish.
4. Cover with a lid or tin foil and bake for 30 minutes. Uncover, stir, and then return to the oven for another 30 minutes.

Serve with hunks of crusty bread and butter.

I always think of December as being a very "foody" month, which I think is common for most people in the northern, western parts of the world. Coming up with a recipe for this month was challenging, therefore, because I didn't want to repeat flavours that I know a lot of us will face over the holiday season. So I settled on this relatively simple and unusual cassoulet-style dish, which uses seasonal parsnips but also incorporates some unseasonal ingredients, as a kind of palate-cleanser between the usual festive fare.

In the home

Traditionally, December has – at least in the northern and western hemisphere – been a month where people have clamoured to bring nature inside, much as we've done throughout this year. From the cutting and laying of the Yule log, to the traditional Christmas tree, through decorating with holly and ivy, and, of course, the hanging of mistletoe, December is a month where nature tangles together in joy and celebration.

Evergreen holly symbolizes good fortune, while ivy represents eternal life and resurrection. Mistletoe, of course, is romance, and who doesn't want a healthy dose of all three to get you through the cold, dark winter months?

So we will do the same. We'll take our last forage outside this year to look for the traditional plants and greenery and, if possible, we'll bring them inside. I personally would caution against ivy, as lovely as it is; it's beloved by spider mites, and once inside they'll seek out your other plants. But holly, mistletoe

and evergreen spruces are welcome, and the latter smells especially lovely.

If pine and spruce are hard to source where you are, consider buying a soy candle with an evergreen fragrance that you can burn to invite the scent of natural winter inside

Cinnamon is a plant too, so a cinnamon cookie or even gingerbread candle wouldn't be amiss.

Mulled wine is the perfect way to bring nature into your home (and tummy), and goes well with a plate of gingerbread or festive cookies. Why not plan an evening in your nest with the scents and flavours of the festive season around you? Look out of the window and up at the winter night sky – do you recognize any of those constellations? What about the Geminids? Will you wish upon a star tonight?

Enjoy the work you've put into this year to make your home a more sustainable and welcoming place for nature.

Check List:

- [ ]
- [ ]
- [ ]
- [ ]
- [ ]
- [ ]
- [ ]
- [ ]

In your phone

The old year is dying and a new one is about to be born, and the natural world will have changed yet again, probably looking very similar to the way it did when you started reading this book. So, this month, let's take our final photos of the year. Let's visit all the spots we've watched grow and change and wax and wane and take their final portraits, for now.

Then, when you're back at home, warm and cozy, scroll back through your year, looking at everything you've recorded, and everything you've done. Think about how having access to this tiny miracle in your pocket has enriched your world, and be glad for all the things it's made possible for you: learning the stars, looking up ingredients, researching seeds and soil, identifying plants, talking to the people you love, making memories you can return to again and again.

We'll come back next year and begin the cycle again.

In caring for yourself

For December, we're going to make a luxe lip balm we can wear when we go outside to protect our lips from the wind and the cold. It's a really quick and simple recipe, and makes an incredible present if you're stuck on last-minute gifts for people.

Homemade luxe lip balm

½ tbsp coconut oil

½ tbsp shea butter

½ tbsp candelilla wax

3-5 drops of essential oil (rose is lovely, but anything fruity would work too)

Small glass pots or tins, 10ml size

Melt the oil, butter and wax together in a heatproof bowl set over a pan of boiling water (or in a microwave) and then stir in the essential oil. Pour into the pots or tins and allow to set.

In writing

Choosing two **Tove Jansson** books could, I suppose, be considered cheating, but I honestly don't give a fig. Besides, *A Winter Book* isn't a novel but a collection of short stories. It's a brief book, and the stories are all a little more fragile than *The Summer Book*. They have an icy, crystalline quality, as though they won't survive the harsh glare of the sun. Each one is introspective and quiet, and a sense of aloneness – not necessarily loneliness – creeps through all of them. If you're a fan of Jansson's work you'll probably notice characters and motifs she uses often: islands, taciturn but good-hearted people, swimming in the water, concerns about the depths.

The book was curated by novelist Ali Smith, and some of the stories within were translated into English for the first time.

The festive season is so full of colour and noise and light and joy, I wonder how much of it we use to distract ourselves from the cold and dark. While it's important sometimes to keep the night at bay, if this year has taught us anything it's that nature is neither good nor bad, and all of it should be embraced with an open heart. Twenty-two short stories means you can easily consume one a day, with room for breaks in between if you need them. There's room for both dark and light, joy and sorrow, company and solitude throughout December, and nothing has context without its opposite. Embrace both sides of your nature this month.

Voices, past and present

December is ridiculously rich with folklore. The hibernal (winter) solstice, the opposite to the midsummer solstice, always happens at some point between the 20th and 23rd of December; another liminal time when the veils between worlds thin and we stand again on the threshold between darkness and light. There are almost as many superstitions about weather, especially on Christmas Day, as there are days in the month. My favourite, though, is a gruesome tale about the price of trickery and hubris, and one that's quite new to me.

Though I have loved the tiny, round, feisty wren all my life, I hadn't heard of Wren Day until I read **The Wren Hunt** by **Mary Watson** and decided to look up the origins of it. Wren Day happens on St Stephen's Day, or Boxing Day to those of us in the UK. In the past, the wren boys would hunt

for a real wren, tearing through the countryside to find one, before tying it to a pole, or trapping it in a net over a pitchfork and parading it through the town, singing songs asking for donations, before culminating in a revelry the whole town takes part in. Thankfully, these days a stuffed wren or some kind of substitute is used.

But why? What can the poor wren have done to deserve such a thing? The answer to that isn't so simple. In fact, tales of the wren's treachery are stitched throughout history.

The wren is the bird blamed for betraying the whereabouts of St Stephen to his enemies, causing him to become the first Christian martyr. It was supposedly a wren that betrayed the presence of Irish soldiers to Viking invaders, by beating its wings on the Irish shields. And it was the wren that later betrayed the Irish again, only this time to Cromwell's soldiers, by taking to the air and waking them from a sleep as the Irish approached. The wren is even mixed up in the assassination of Julius Caesar – apparently, a wren carrying a sprig of laurel in its beak was attacked and killed in the Roman senate by a group of other birds the day before!

The most popular story about the wickedness of the wren is attributed to Aesop, and it goes like this...

Once upon a time, God wanted to know who the king of the birds was and so he set a challenge that whichever one could fly the highest would be crowned the king. One by one the birds all dropped away, until it seemed the eagle would win. Only for a tiny wren, hidden in the eagle's feathers to shoot out and fly higher, claiming the title. But because no one likes a trickster, the poor wren was forced to pay for its crimes, year after year, at the wren hunt.

It's a typically grisly fable, warning of the dangers of trying to cheat and maybe also aiming too high. But it's also a tale about adapting, and thinking on your feet, and turning a situation to your advantage when the odds are against you. Yes, once a year the wren was hunted for its crime, but the rest of the time it was still the king of the birds, and death on St Stephen's Day wasn't certain – only if it was caught. I like the wren; it's a scrappy little bird, both in the real world and the folkloric one, always looking for a way to come out on top.

In a nice act of serendipity, for the briefest second I see a wren as I'm finishing up my chat with December's interviewee, Misha Anker. I want very much to hold it in my hands and feels its speeding bird heart against my fingers, but almost as soon as I've thought it, the wren is gone, flitting back to the crevices and low spaces it prefers and from which it draws its Latin name: *troglodytes troglodytes*. Probably for the best; who knows how it might betray me if I drew its attention…

A second piece of serendipity occurs when I find out Misha, a 28-year-old theatre technician, is from the same city I grew up in. It's a joyous, magical moment, because it's the first time I've met someone who understands precisely the strange blend of boringly suburban and enticingly rural that was my childhood, and how a walk of just minutes can take you from a place that's wholly human to very wild. Coventry conjures up images of concrete jungle, but it's not my experience of it. And it's not Misha's either.

It means our chat quickly deviates into local legends we both heard growing up, including the various big cats that were supposed to haunt almost every scrap of open space in the town. Neither of us ever saw one. Neither of us ever stopped wanting to.

Misha describes herself as an Enid Blyton child: "There was a lot of playing in the river and climbing trees and finding things, eating wild gooseberries and seeing what happened. I have a relatively early memory of my mother teaching me about poisonous flowers, because I liked to make what I called petal perfume, putting petals in an old margarine tub full of water where they would slowly go rancid."

Her parents encouraged her to engage with nature; she recalls one summer being given a faunarium – a small plastic tank with a vented roof – and catching caterpillars to watch them metamorphose, and another summer convincing her mother to build a pond in the garden to house frogspawn her grandmother brought to her.

After a period living and working in London, it was a move back to the countryside with her now ex-wife that began rewilding her. She talks about wanting to actively engage with nature, instead of just observing it casually, and how the further away she's got from formal education the more she's realized that learning for fun can be – well, fun!

"In the past year or so I've been really making an effort to try to learn some of the stuff. I love the idea of being able to say, 'yes – *this* is this edible plant', or 'that jolly yellow thing is called *this*.'"

This period of learning and reflecting has left Misha feeling she notices the turn of the seasons more, mentioning the produce in shops – something she hadn't especially paid attention to while she lived in the city – and how she sees that changing in tandem with the fields near her home. In her old home she had an allotment and she talks about the satisfaction of the process of growing her own food, taking it from soil to plate, and how she misses it, though she still grows things in pots.

"There's something enormously satisfying about coming home with dirt under your fingernails and knowing you made things grow. There was nothing there and now there's a plant," she says. And I know the feeling, because it's how I feel too – it's what drives me to fill my windowsills with boxes and pots of earth and grow whatever I can. The idea of being there from beginning to end, of seeing the whole process through.

The latest skill Misha is trying to master from the start is spinning her own wool. The morning we speak she's just taken a delivery of a drop spindle from Etsy and has a sample of fleece to spin on it. And a friend's mother keeps a small flock of sheep and has promised her a fleece of unwashed wool. From there, the plan is to eventually knit a jumper from the wool she's washed, carded and spun herself.

It makes me furiously jealous, and – despite my veganism – want to do the same. The idea of taking something from its rawest state and turning it into a finished product is the thing that pleases me most of all – from writing books, to gardening, to cooking. And it seems Misha feels the same way. That the cycle, and the completion of the cycle – whether the seasons, the harvest, or even the clothes we wear – is something to be treasured.

December

In your hands

Acknowledgements

Writing this book felt like an act of serendipity, coming along at exactly the right time, and it will always hold a special place in my heart because of it. As will the many, many people who helped bring such a joyful project to life.

Endless thank-yous to:

My editor Ella Chappell, who guided this book with both innate wisdom and perfect understanding of what I wanted it to be;

Ella Tjader for the most beautiful illustrations, translating my words into art;

The marketing and publicity team at Watkins for wanting to make this book soar; Rachel Gladman, Isabelle Panay, Laura Whitaker-Jones and Fizza Nayer;

The amazing people who allowed me to interview them about their relationships with nature: Louisa Adjoa Parker, Misha Anker, Alice Broadway, Laura Elliott, Lizzie Huxley-Jones, Catherine Johnson, Emilie Lyons, Katie Marsden Anna McKerrow and Kiran Millwood Hargrave;

Biologist Katie G. Garrett, who filled in the gaps of my knowledge about flora and fauna in the United States;

Acknowledgements

Everyone behind the scenes at Watkins: those who checked I had my moons and stars in the right places at the right times, the copy-editors who helped shape this into something readable, the designers and production staff who made it look so beautiful, and to everyone who worked on it without me ever knowing. I appreciate you even if I don't know you. And Daniel Culver, for being so patient with my nit-picking edits;

My agent, Claire Wilson, for letting me have this one;

And finally, to my friends and family, who all saw this coming. Thank you for listening to me bang on about nature; hopefully writing this will have got some of it out of my system.

Index

Index